LIFE ON THE EDGE

Extreme Adventures of
TROY HENKELS

TELEGRAPH HERALD

THONLINE.COM

a division of Woodward Communications, Inc.

Dubuque, Iowa

TELEGRAPH HERALD
THonline.com
Dubuque, Iowa

Publisher: James F. Normandin
Editor: Brian Cooper
Director: Jeff Wolff
Project Coordinator: Diane Mohr
Cover/Interior Design: Kathleen Hoeper
Cover Photo: © Laurent Dick/www.sailantarctica.com

ISBN 978-0-9819806-5-2

Printed in the United States of America

For my Father who,
without knowing it,
made me realize long ago,
that chasing dreams
results in a life well spent.

Contents

Acknowledgments

This book would have never been possible if it weren't for the characters and expedition partners that I have had the honor to accompany on trips all over the world. Thanks to them, with duffel bags full of gear and memories, I have always returned home safe and sound: Dave Klavitter, Brady Fink, Dan "Danimal" Corroon, Collins Gilbertson, Matt Rucando, Seth "Chuck" Young, Ford Reeves, Jeff King, Sam Gehring, the Global Extremes team, Jon Gauti, Dave "Smitty" Smith, Luke Davis, Mikey, Doug Stroop, Dani Evenson, Julie Brown, Rumen Grozev, Laurent Dick, Pieterjan Kempynck, Frans Doomen, Michel Tordoir, Tracy Stiehr, the NBQ team, Geza Scholtz, Bjorn Detre, and Jason Turnbull.
Thanks also to the best sponsors in the world: Oakley, Kōkatat and Ozone.

Without the great staff at the Telegraph Herald this book would not have been a reality. Thanks to James Normandin, Diane Mohr, David Kettering, Kathleen Hoeper and Jeff Wolff. And Brian Cooper, who had the vision to bring this project to light and whose hard work made it possible.

And thanks to:

All the friends and family who unwaveringly offered words of encouragement, interest, and support for so many years: Laddie Shaw, Bill Ross, Claire Donahue, Dave Calkins, Todd & Ginnie Henkels, Terry Henkels, Trudy & Neil Hancock, Jan Houser, Mary Lee Stiehr, Dan Richard, Rob Mancuso, Kathy Calhoun, John Sutter, Scott Bowers, Lance Jordt, Bill Hicks, Russ Madigan, Mark Truax, Todd Lowery, Liz Lasater, Brenda Martakis, Suzie Brown, Charlie Varley, Joe White, John Cantalupo, Jody Vanderah, Dale Frommelt, Kevin "Moose" Clemens, Dave Johnson, Larry Kemp, Susan Dunsmore, Kara and Denny Vance, Ron and Janine Niebrugge, Harry and Susan Ernst, Andi Parrett, Mike Schmalz, Dan Schmalz, Tom Straka, Vicki Malone, and Leesa Tomlin. And thanks to all the family and friends, who are too many to mention that have supported my endeavors for so many years.

Dixie Dansercoer for providing me with opportunities and experiences that come along few times in life. His friendship and expedition partnership have been invaluable.

Robert Waller for being a mentor and friend. He helped me realize early on that you only get one chance at life, you better make it worthwhile.

Maggie Kelly for always being there with love, encouragement and support no matter the circumstances or how wild the idea.

My Father, for his interest and enthusiasm. He is the one who most often tells me I'm crazy, but I believe he would have seized the same opportunities, with energy, had he been given them in his younger years.

"You don't have to be a fantastic hero to do certain things — to compete. You can be just an ordinary chap, sufficiently motivated."

- Edmund Hillary

Preface

Growing up on an apple orchard outside Dubuque, Iowa, was nothing short of special. Little did I realize in those days that I had it made. Every day was spent out of doors, either in the orchard or exploring the local county roads, as far as my bike would carry me. It was a small world, and there were few opportunities to venture out into the bigger world. Nonetheless, from an early age I had a strong sense of curiosity. After long bike rides or forays in my Grandpa's timber, I was always anxious to return to the woods for more exploring.

My happiest moments were spent outside. As you might imagine, with six kids growing up in the country, we spent most of our time out of doors, no matter the season.

After a normal progression through high school and college, I found myself in a career job in Kansas City. I spent long days at the office, and hundred-hour work weeks were the norm. This was certainly not how I wanted to live my life. But the overhead of two weeks of vacation time, health insurance, and a retirement plan seemed too overwhelming and important to give up. By chance, a childhood friend decided to spend a summer in Alaska. It was a place that had always intrigued me, and I was green with envy. So I used a precious week of vacation time and flew to Alaska. It turned out to be like no place I'd ever been before. Wild, remote, unexplored, vast, and few people. I was enthralled and could not wait to return.

A year later, I quit my job. It was one of the most difficult and taxing decisions I'd ever made. Without knowing it at the time, it was a decision that would forever change the course of my life. I realized it was time to chase down my dreams before I was too old and left wondering where life had gone.

Giving up a corporate job in the city seemed a like a good tradeoff to having the opportunity to see Alaska. So, I packed up my 1983 Subaru station wagon and drove for a week, across Canada, to Alaska. It was the farthest I had ever been from home. With $5,000 in the bank, I imagined I would return to a "real" job when the money ran out. The summer was spent living, working, and exploring Denali National Park. At summer's end, much to my surprise, I hadn't spent my savings but had saved $5,000 more. I then realized that I could live and work in an amazing environment and actually survive and make money. From that point on, I never again entertained the idea of moving back to a city or pursuing a "real" job.

Summers were spent in Denali Park and winters were spent traveling and living in the places that I had always dreamed of. The first winter, I worked and skied in the mountains of Colorado. Having always wanted to experience the tropics, I spent the next three winters on St. John in the Virgin Islands. Eventually, Antarctica caught my eye and I ended up spending 16 months working and living there. Finally, Alaska ended up being home, where I now spend my life year-round. My roots are still in Iowa, but my love affair with Alaska has gone on unwaveringly for 20 years.

In Alaska, I built on the foundation skills learned in Boy Scouts and growing up in the country. My first adventures were no different than back home: hiking, biking and camping, but this time it was in the backcountry of Denali National Park. Before long, my walks turned into 12-hour hikes. Backpacking trips turned into climbing trips. I started ice climbing and paragliding. Climbing trips turned into full-on expeditions. My skill set was built over time and with experience. Without knowing it, this was a necessary apprenticeship before I was able to head to the remote corners of the planet to test my mettle against nature, mountains, and the elements. It never occurred to me that anything I did would result in stories that could be published in a book that the general public might enjoy reading. For me, the experiences are just what I do, a part of my everyday life.

I am fortunate to have had some unique and special adventures. I hope you enjoy reading about them as much as I had living them.

Troy Henkels
Eagle River, Alaska
henkeltr@yahoo.com
TroyHenkels.com

FOLLOW TROY'S ADVENTURES:

Source: *The World Factbook*

Denali National Park
★ Wales
U.S.
★ Eagle River
★ Seward

Alcan trip route

CANADA

Dubuque ★
Moab ★
Aspen ★
UNITED STATES

Phoenix ★
BMW motorcycle trip route

Mazatlan ★ MEXICO
Acapulco ★
Puerto Escondido ★
Panajachel ★

GUATEMALA HONDURAS
EL SALVADOR NICARAGUA
COSTA RICA

Panama Canal
Santa Clara ★ Panama City
Darién Jungle

VENEZUELA
COLOMBIA
ECUADOR
PERU
BOLIVIA
PARAGUAY

BRAZIL

CHILE
Aconcagua ★
ARGENTINA
URUGUAY

Torres del Paine ★
Punta Arenas ★ Strait of Magellan
Ushuaia ★

Drake Passage
Antarctic Peninsula

Ross Ice Shelf
Siple Dome ★

Greenland (DENMARK)

Isafjodur ★ ★ ICELAND
Reykjavik ★ Hvannadalshnjku

NORTH ATLANTIC OCEAN

SOUTH ATLANTIC OCEAN

NORTH PACIFIC OCEAN

SOUTH PACIFIC OCEAN

SOUTHERN OCEAN

FOLLOW TROY'S ADVENTURES:

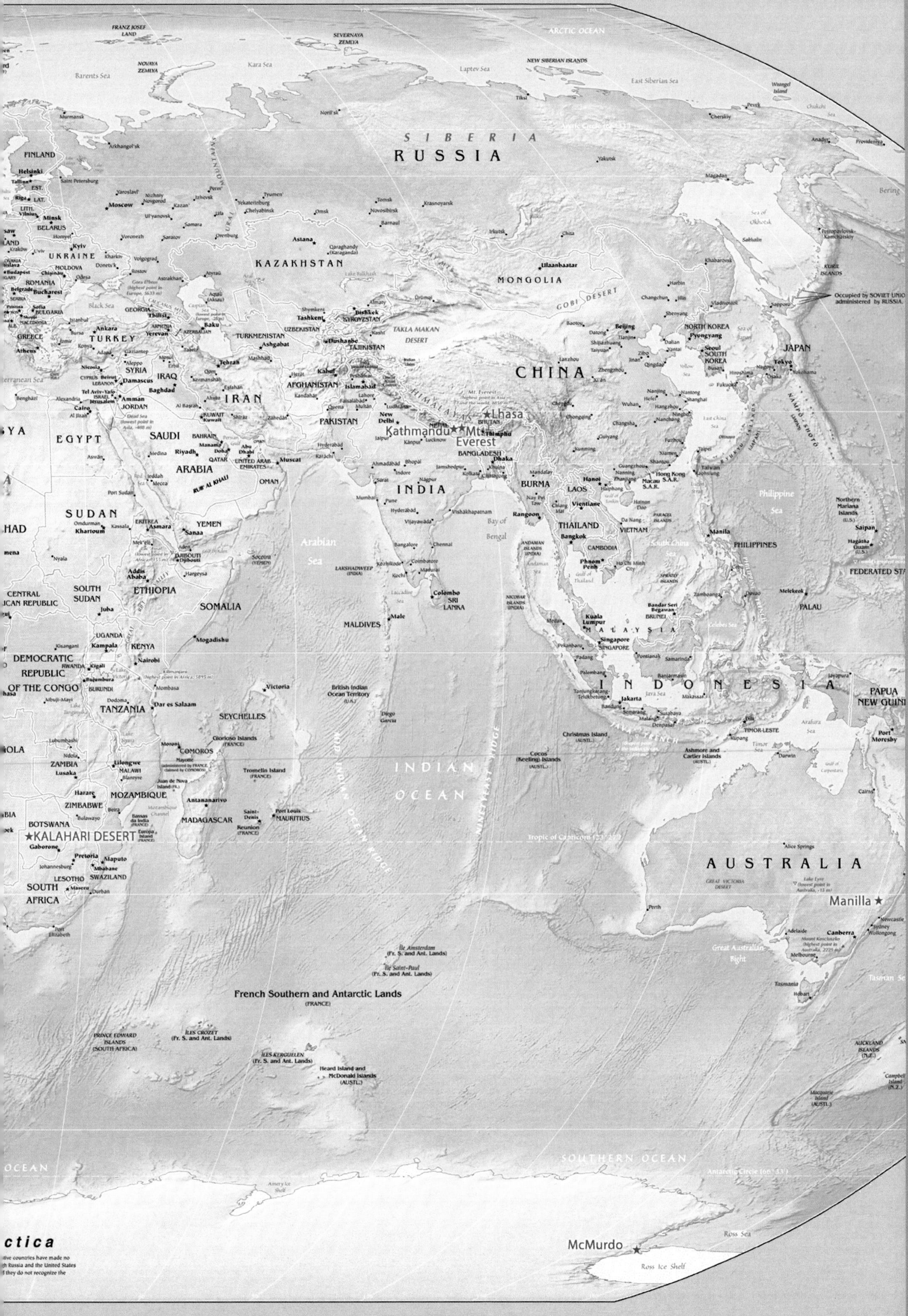

North Pacific
Ocean

Bering Sea

Bristol
Bay

Kamchatskiy

Petropavlovsk

Kodiak
Harding
Icefield
Bethel
Providentiya
Anadyr'
Maga

Gulf of
Iditarod
Trail
Nome
King
Island
KOLYMSKOYE NAGOR'YE

Zaliv
Shelikhova

Seward
Anchorage
Eagle River
Valdez
Denali
Moose's Tooth
Wales
Bering
Strait
Kolyma

Pioneer
Peak
Fireweed
Race
UNITED STATES
Chukchi
Sea
RUSSIA
Oy

Juneau

Whitehorse
Fairbanks
Peyek
Cherskiy
Verk

Dawson
Yukon River
BROOKS RANGE

MOUNTAINS
lson
Wrangel
Island
East
Siberian
Sea
Til

MACKENZIE
MOUNTAINS
Prudhoe
Bay
Barrow

Mackenzie River
Inuvik
Beaufort
Sea
sea ice extent
summer average
2000-2006
NEW
SIBERIAN
ISLANDS
Verk

Yellowknife

Great Bear
Lake

Great Slave
Lake
Banks
Island
Arctic
Ocean
Laptev
Sea

Cambridge
Bay
Victoria
Island
SEVERNAYA
ZEMLYA

CANADA
QUEEN
ELIZABETH
ISLANDS
North
Pole
North Bound Quest
Expedition
Kar
Sea

viat
Gjoa
Haven
Resolute
Ellesmere
Island
Alert
Barneo
FRANZ
JOSEF
LAND

Repulse
Bay
Pond
Inlet
Qaanaaq
(Thule)
Nord
NOVAYA
ZEMLYA

Baffin
Island
Baffin
Bay
Spitsbergen
(NORWAY)
Longyearbyen

Iqaluit
Molloy Deep
(deepest point of
Arctic Ocean,
-5607 m)
Barents Sea

uaq
Greenland
(DENMARK)
Greenland
Sea

Davis Strait
Ilulissat
(Jakobshavn)
Bjørnøya
(NORWAY)

Sisimiut
(Holsteinsborg)
Nuuk
(Godthåb)

abrador
Sea
Ittoqqortoormiit
(Scoresbysund)
Jan Mayen
(NORWAY)
Murm

Qaqortoq
(Julianehåb)
Tasiilaq

Denmark Strait
Norwegian
Sea

Arctic Circle

Reykjavik
ICELAND
NORWAY
FINLAN

Source: *The World Factbook*

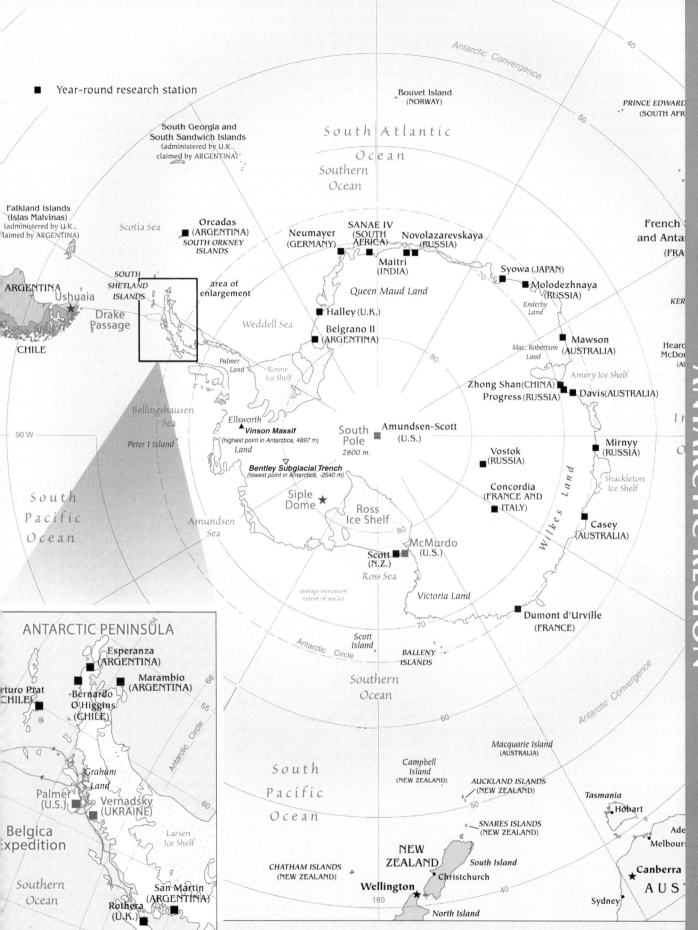

■ Year-round research station

Bouvet Island
(NORWAY)

PRINCE EDWARD
(SOUTH AFR

South Georgia and
South Sandwich Islands
(administered by U.K.,
claimed by ARGENTINA)

South Atlantic
Ocean
Southern
Ocean

Falkland Islands
(Islas Malvinas)
(administered by U.K.,
claimed by ARGENTINA)

Scotia Sea

Orcadas
(ARGENTINA)
SOUTH ORKNEY
ISLANDS

Neumayer
(GERMANY)

SANAE IV
(SOUTH
AFRICA)

Novolazarevskaya
(RUSSIA)

French
and Anta
(FRA

Maitri
(INDIA)

Syowa (JAPAN)

Molodezhnaya
(RUSSIA)

KER

ARGENTINA
Ushuaia

SOUTH
SHETLAND
ISLANDS

area of
enlargement

Queen Maud Land

Enderby
Land

Drake
Passage

Halley (U.K.)

Weddell Sea

Belgrano II
(ARGENTINA)

Mawson
(AUSTRALIA)

Mac. Robertson
Land

Heard
McDo
(AU

CHILE

Palmer
Land

Ronne
Ice Shelf

Amery Ice Shelf

Zhong Shan(CHINA)
Progress (RUSSIA)

Davis(AUSTRALIA)

Bellingshausen
Sea

Ir

90 W

Peter 1 Island

Ellsworth

Vinson Massif
(highest point in Antarctica, 4897 m)
Land

South
Pole
2800 m.

Amundsen-Scott
(U.S.)

Vostok
(RUSSIA)

Mirnyy
(RUSSIA)

Shackleton
Ice Shelf

O

Bentley Subglacial Trench
(lowest point in Antarctica, -2540 m)

Concordia
(FRANCE AND
ITALY)

Wilkes Land

Casey
(AUSTRALIA)

South
Pacific
Ocean

Amundsen
Sea

Siple
Dome

Ross
Ice Shelf

80

McMurdo
(U.S.)

Scott
(N.Z.)

Ross Sea

average minimum
extent of sea ice

Victoria Land

Dumont d'Urville
(FRANCE)

70

Scott
Island

Antarctic   Circle

BALLENY
ISLANDS

Southern
Ocean

60

Antarctic Convergence

Macquarie Island
(AUSTRALIA)

Campbell
Island
(NEW ZEALAND)

AUCKLAND ISLANDS
(NEW ZEALAND)

Tasmania

Hobart

South
Pacific
Ocean

50

SNARES ISLANDS
(NEW ZEALAND)

Ade
Melbour

CHATHAM ISLANDS
(NEW ZEALAND)

NEW
ZEALAND

South Island

Christchurch

Canberra

AUS

Wellington

180

40

Sydney

North Island

Source: The World Factbook

ANTARCTIC PENINSULA

Esperanza
(ARGENTINA)

Marambio
(ARGENTINA)

rturo Prat
CHILE

Bernardo
O'Higgins
(CHILE)

Graham
Land

Palmer
(U.S.)

Vernadsky
(UKRAINE)

Belgica
Expedition

Larsen
Ice Shelf

Southern
Ocean

San Martin
(ARGENTINA)

Rothera
(U.K.)

ANTARCTIC REGION

L-R: Father Joe, Troy, and brothers Todd, Terry (front center).   © Pete Henkels

CHAPTER ONE

IT'S NEVER TOO LATE

When I was young, I had great respect and reverence for my elders. My grandfather's life was one of hard work on the farm. Typically in our family, that generation would not have even thought of spending time or money on traveling the world for adventure. Everyday challenges were enough adventure for most in that day and age.

My great uncle, Father Joe, was different. Grandpa's brother, he spent 23 years as a missionary in China – something unheard of then or now. I drew inspiration from his stories of bicycling through rice paddies and evading the Japanese army in World War II. By the time I knew Father Joe, he was old, but somehow he never lost his spirit for living a vivid life and enjoying nature, even though his focus changed from international to local adventure. I could always find him at Divine Word College seminary in Epworth, Iowa, tending his gardens and orchard. In the winter, he read about China and practiced on his ancient violin. He always took the time to share his experiences, telling stories that intrigued me to explore. Though I didn't realize it at the time, Father Joe was my hero, and someone I greatly respected and admired. His impact on me was such that during my teenage years I even considered becoming a priest; that adventure still eludes me.

In my youth, my father demanded respect just by the way he went about life and how he involved himself as a father of six children. He was always passionate in his pursuits – growing apples, coaching youth baseball, creating fireplace doors, or designing and building contraptions. He gets an idea in his head and makes it happen. I remember once finding him at his lathe in the garage, giddy with excitement. When I asked what he was making, he replied, "A cannon." He had an idea and so he made it. That cannon was the source of great fun and noise when I was young, and even

until this day. The list of things my father has accomplished is endless and no matter what, he approaches them with a passion I have observed in few people.

These role models served me well over the years. After college I made a vow to myself to not let life pass me by, but to live it to the fullest. In no way did I want to wake up one day and be 80 years old, thinking of all the things I'd wished I'd done. I was going to do them and I was going to do them right! After several years trying my hand at the typical American dream and holding down a "real job," it dawned on me that I was losing sight of my pledge. So I set out for a life of uncertainty and adventure in Alaska. Although there have been tradeoffs, this approach to living life has served me well. It has taken me, in odd ways, all over the world, and on all sorts of adventures. I've been to places that in my youth seemed too many miles and too many years away to even dream about. Standing on top of Mount McKinley, shivering at the South Pole, warming up on beaches in the Virgin Islands, and trying to catch my breath on Mount Everest are not experiences I could have fit into a two-week vacation from a corporate job.

As I get older, I wonder whether this must change at some point. Can a person ever fulfill all of his dreams? I think of my elders and the way they lived and their tenacity to stay true to themselves. And I am reminded of a few people who have impressed me along the way. On Denali, I met a 60-year-old climber who was just looking to finish the last chapter of his climbing career by summiting. On Everest, I met a 72-year-old climber with a goal to reach the top, a place he had stood 18 years earlier. Sitting in base camp at Everest, I realized that it is never too late to live life. It doesn't really matter if those older guys reach the summit of some mountain. What matters is that they are still out

Blue Bell Orchard, Dubuque, Iowa.   *© Troy Henkels*

there trying, living life, and pursuing their own dreams.

Years ago I was sidelined with a broken arm from a paragliding mishap. That experience reminded me of how short life can be and how quickly it can change or be taken away. My thoughts were that maybe someday my focus will change, and maybe I will slow down. But you can bet I'll do exactly what my elders have done. Just like Father Joe did for his 96 years and as my own father has done for 76 years. He's still growing apples and living life to the fullest – every day. Because of them, I know it's never too late to start pursuing the dreams we have in life.

CHAPTER TWO

RIDING ON THE EDGE

I started being an explorer at a very early age. It was never enough to go only as far as I could see. I had to go over the next hill – and the next, and the next – knowing full well if I explored forever, I would never see it all. Countless days of my youth were spent exploring the back roads and backwoods of Dubuque County. Fortunately, my parents recognized this, and moved our family to the country. There might have been other reasons, but I like to think they were looking to satisfy my thirst for exploring, and they knew I just wouldn't be content growing up in town. Whatever the reason, I was happy to be raised in the country with plenty of places to roam and explore.

Judging from the maps, I wasn't even sure the trip could be accomplished. But I knew from the start that I had to try. For more than 10 years I concocted backcountry adventures around Alaska. For me, they were exploratory forays into a wilderness untouched and unpopulated by man, where weather patterns and wildlife rule the landscape. In typical fashion, I envisioned a route through a section of wilderness I had not yet explored, nor could I find anyone who had. My focus was a remote area just north of Denali National Park. The trip would take me through an area too remote to be easily accessible on foot. It was a recipe I had used often in the Alaskan wilderness: set off into the unknown, alone, traveling light, and going far. I would push the limits of endurance, distance, and daylight. Part of the allure was to see how far I could get into the wilderness and back out again in a day, utilizing Alaska's long hours of daylight.

However, this trip would be different. I wanted to mountain bike 40 to 60 miles into the bush using old mining roads and river drainages to make a large loop from my starting point back to an active highway. However, in Alaska, things don't always work out as planned. For safety reasons, on this trip I would need a capable partner. The distances were just too great to take a chance of going solo and risking a problem. An accident 60 miles into the Alaskan bush can spell disaster – oftentimes death. I have never been one to avoid risks; I actually welcome them. But this would be one of those trips where caution was necessary.

While spending the summer in Denali National Park, I started searching for a partner. Brady, a lively 23-year-old, who was rarely seen without his bike, was my first choice. I figured if he was on his bike all the time, he must be in good enough shape to ride 60 miles, off-road, in a single day.

My approach to Brady was subtle. I mentioned my idea, unsure what his reaction would be. He beamed at the suggestion and said to count him in. This, despite my warnings of a very long day, barely navigable terrain, river crossings, and deep wilderness. This just spurred him on, which was exactly the reaction I was hoping for.

In early July, we drive the first 30 miles to our takeoff spot at the road's end. We anticipate exploring some extremely remote backcountry and know it will be one long day on our bikes. Before we even start, we are already 30

Troy and Brady, deep in the Alaska wilderness.

© Troy Henkels

Boot Hill with Jumbo Dome and the Alaska Range in the background.

Brady making a river crossing.

miles into the bush. Brady, like any young guy, takes off down the first hill at breakneck speed, despite my advice to set a pace that he could maintain hour after hour. Being in my early 30s, I am considered the "old man" and Brady the one who is "young and inexperienced." By the first steep uphill, Brady is walking his bike as I roll by, riding at a slow, steady pace. From that point on, Brady understands: It is going to be a very long day of biking.

We ride under a sunny sky and warm temperatures, a real treat in the interior of Alaska. The trail takes us through an old coal mining district that is seldom visited and threads us over rolling hills with views of all the surrounding peaks … Sugarloaf, Jumbo Dome, Pete's Peak -- which I climbed and subsequently named for my father, which is a story for another time – and Mount Dora. This area is so immense it seems like you can look to the horizon and imagine it never ending. It has Brady and me feeling a bit overwhelmed, yet I am thrilled to explore places that to me were previously only topographic lines on a map.

The trail turns and twists us 15 miles deeper into the Alaskan bush. As the trail descends into a river valley, it becomes a bit more obscure. We pass remnants of early mining days. We will cross countless rivers on this journey; this I know from studying the maps. So the first is no surprise when we dip into the frigid waters. Fortunately, the weather is kind and the rivers are running low. Even so, several river crossings challenge our physical stamina by almost sweeping us away.

© Troy Henkels

The trail conditions change under wheel each time we climb out of a stream. Often, I resort to the topographic map to figure our route, and realize the only way to get to where we hope to go is to follow the river, which in turn becomes our trail. With numb toes, we press on, deeper into the wilderness.

The area we travel through is considered the Liberty Bell Mining District. Although there are still mining claims in the area, there is little active mining. Most of the mining was done in the 1940s and 1950s. To our surprise in one birch-lined river valley, we come across several homesteads, where active gold mining is taking place using the old methods. Several families live out here with little contact to the outside world. I'm deeply impressed that a family can

survive the hardships of the Alaska bush, so far away from modern conveniences. The children seem happily content to be playing in the wilderness and we, on our bikes, seem to be a bit of a novelty to them: Few visitors ever make it this far into the wilderness because of the dangerous river crossings. This family is very helpful. They give us much-needed information on directions and upcoming crossings. With that, we travel on, not really knowing what to expect.

By the time we reach the big rivers, I'm tired and Brady is exhausted. Crossing the Totatlanika turns out to be extremely challenging in the thigh-deep, chilly, swift-moving water. We shoulder the bikes and, fortunately, make the crossing without incident. With more than 20 miles still left to go, we gradually cross California Creek and Eva Creek. They are less challenging but just as bone-chilling. As we find better trail and more recent mining remnants from the 1960s, we climb out of the valleys and above tree line. More than one spot offers us spectacular views of snow-covered Denali (Mount McKinley) soaring in the distance, more than 100 miles away. It's a fine reward to all the miles traveled in the lowlands.

The last difficult climb takes us to Boot Hill. A cemetery of sorts used by generations of local miners and their families as repose for their worn-out boots. It's certainly an oddity of humanity in this pristine wilderness. With relief, we begin the 10-mile descent back to the road system. Our last highlight is passing though "Windy City," an area that is home to some very large dilapidated pieces of heavy mining equipment and even heavier winds. It's known for its wind, and today is no exception, as we are buffeted with 30-knot gusts.

By day's end, Brady and I have traveled more than 50 miles. On the drive home, we talk about how simply beautiful this ride turned out to be. It's hard to grasp how remote we really were, just in the course of one day. For me, it was no different than the days of my youth exploring the rolling hills of Iowa. I know now, as I did then, if I hadn't dreamed of what was beyond the next hill, I would have never explored there. So, I'm left wondering what is beyond the next hill in Alaska and life.

On the flanks of Mount Alice before attempting to reach the summit.

© Dave Haney

CHAPTER THREE

ONE STEP AT A TIME UP MOUNT ALICE

Looking at Mount Alice from across the bay in Seward, Alaska, is a daunting sight, to say the least. This mountain rises 5,265 feet above Resurrection Bay and is the highest peak in the area. It is named after one of the Lowell daughters, an early settler in the area.

One must understand the difficulties and dangers of this climb. Mount Alice is a mass of vertical rock that rises abruptly and is surrounded by the ocean on one side and glaciers on all other sides. The rock is not granite, but shale and therefore very poor for climbing safely. This "rotten rock" is despised in the climbing world because it breaks off and crumbles when a climber grabs onto it. It offers no secure placement of anchors to arrest a fall. Another major problem is the weather. This part of Alaska experiences very few sunny days, and typically the weather changes rapidly into rain, fog, and wind. These factors combined offer very little in the way of hope of standing on top of this mountain.

My failed attempts at climbing Mount Alice were starting to add up. While climbing just about every other mountain in the area, I studied possible routes up Mount Alice and couldn't see an easy way up. The perplexing thing was, I couldn't find anyone who had been up Mount Alice in summer. I talked to one person who had barely made it to the top in winter by climbing near vertical snow chutes on the west face. Even historical records listed people who had tried over the years, and only mentioned those who died trying. There was not one listing of anyone making it to the top.

My aspirations to climb this mountain had not been for lack of effort. Six years earlier, a climbing buddy (appropriately nicknamed Danimal) and I made an attempt. Danimal is one of the few people I would trust on such dangerous terrain. He was experienced in the mountains and willing to take some calculated risks. In sunny weather, we made our approach and even got part way across the long

knife ridge that leads to the real climbing and eventually the summit. But the weather deteriorated quickly and a heavy drizzle, coupled with dense fog, put us scrambling on slick rock to get back to safety. The hike down took hours as we navigated ridgelines and dense woods in the heavy fog. We got disoriented and actually got lost more than a few times. It was very much like hiking in the dark without a flashlight.

Despite my previous failed attempts, I set out again on a rare crystal-clear day with no wind. My friend Dave accompanies me for the approach hike until the real climbing starts. He is content to soak up the sun in a large field of alpine flowers and wait for me to return.

The approach hike is an Alaskan classic. The trail traverses through dense spruce forests choked with alders and a particularly nasty thorny plant called "devils club." Hiking up from sea level through this strata of vegetation, I'm quaintly reminded of the dense rainforests of Australia and Central America. Certainly, this part of Alaska boasts some of the densest forest vegetation anywhere in the state. Once above tree line, the trail continues upward along a rocky spine that offers spectacular views of Resurrection Bay, the surrounding mountains, and the crevasse-riddled glaciers below. Dave and I make the final hike up extremely large boulders to a wide-open expanse that abruptly ends in a cascade of rock that plummets straight down to the spectacular Godwin Glacier, several thousand feet below. This is where Dave stops and climbing begins in earnest. Dave wishes me luck and reclines to take a nap in the sun.

With no ropes or protective climbing gear, I plan to move quickly and be back in three hours. The climb begins with a long traverse across a knife ridge that leads to more vertical rock and will eventually lead me to the summit. This ridge becomes narrower and more daunting the farther I go. It is bad enough that one slip or mistake will

Mount Alice, left of center, with Seward and Resurrection Bay below.
© Troy Henkels

Standing on the summit of Mount Alice.

© Troy Henkels

send me plummeting down either side of the ridge to the glaciers below, but the rock offers no sense of safety on the continuous ups and downs of the ridgeline. Finally, sweating and breathing heavily, I manage my way to a small saddle between the ridge and the main wall of rock that rises almost vertically above me, all the way to the summit. Along the ridge I stop several times to study this mass of rock to see if I can find a reasonable way to climb it. From this vantage point I don't see a safe way to the top, and several times I consider turning back. But my curiosity always gets the best of me and I have to at least go have a look.

Looking up from the saddle, I am unsure where to go.

The rock is all fairly vertical and in bad shape. I decide to try a route to the right, thinking if I can just get past this section, I ought to be able to get to the top. Several precarious moves later, I am above the worst of it and I continue climbing. Before long, I come across another spot that seems impossible. I find a way through this section as well. After one more tricky section, I think I will be at the top. No such luck. I continue on and on through a seemingly endless array of vertical rock.

After the fourth false summit and another difficult pitch, I realize what was happening. Looking at Mount Alice from across the Bay, reaching the summit seemed impossible. But,

28

taking each pitch individually, I was getting up the mountain, one step at a time. After several more dangerous pitches, I finally stand on the top.

Filled with euphoria that only comes from accomplishing a challenging and risky task, I wonder if Dave can see me. I take in the expansive view of mountains, glaciers, and ocean, all in one sweeping glance. In the sunny weather this is one of the most beautiful places I have ever been. However, my thoughts soon become occupied with getting down safely. Climbing up had been difficult, yet I knew I was only halfway finished with this mountain. After fifteen minutes, I start the descent. The same formula for climbing up would work for going down. Each pitch presents its own puzzle. After each is solved, I can move on to the next pitch. Before long, I am back at the saddle, looking up at what I had just covered. The traverse back across the long knife ridgeline is uneventful yet challenging after the exertion of hours of climbing.

When I meet up with Dave, he is a bit apprehensive. He had heard rock falling off the mountain as I was going up and down, but he could not see me on the rock face. He had spotted me on the summit, so he knew I had at least made it up without mishap.

After several hours, we are back at sea level, looking up at Mount Alice. It still looks impossible to climb. Reflecting on that climb, I realized that climbing mountains is no different than living life. By taking it one step at a time, you get to where you want to be. Everyone has their own mountains to climb, every day. Be it raising kids, getting through college, ascending the corporate ladder, buying a house, or climbing mountains, it all works the same. For me, I'll stick to the easy stuff, and keep climbing mountains in Alaska.

The race trail up Mount Marathon.   © Ron Niebrugge/www.wildnatureimages.com

CHAPTER FOUR

GOING THE DISTANCE ON THE FOURTH OF JULY

Every Fourth of July during my childhood was spent in very traditional ways: hot summer days filled with picnics, baseball, ice cream socials at Eagle Point Park, and fireworks exploding in the sky above the Mississippi River. In those days, I never dreamed of doing anything else on July 4. What else could be better? Since then, I've been around the world, and have spent July 4 in some very unimaginable ways.

On the Fourth, McMurdo Station has a celebration of sorts, and I had the privilege to play in the world's southernmost rock band during the deep, cold darkness of an Antarctic winter. There were no fireworks, just a crew of hardy Americans on the fringe of a continent celebrating a holiday that seemed a world away. The band played to that lively bunch on the bed of a flatbed trailer in the mechanic shop.

During a Fourth of July in Iowa, there are tractor pulls. In Denali Park, Alaska, the locals throw a festival complete with dunk tank, dog cycle races, and a dog pull. In Alaska on this day, the dogs do the pulling and often pull in excess of 3,000 pounds. If that weren't enough, dog teams race, pulling a motorless motorcycle and driver on a teeth-rattling mile-long course. Being the driver in several such races left me marveling at how differently people celebrate this day. Since I moved north, I've come to realize the Fourth of July traditions of my boyhood days in Dubuque have slowly been replaced by unusual Alaska traditions.

I thought I had seen it all until I moved to Seward, Alaska. Seward is a small community (population 3,000) that is home to Kenai Fjords National Park. I'd spent several years in and around Seward, exploring the park, mountains, and ocean. It is a stunning sight, where the mountains rise up thousands of feet from the sea. Seward is home to the Mount Marathon race, which has been run every July 4 since 1915. It is the second-oldest footrace in the country, next to the

Boston Marathon. But don't let the name deceive you. This race is not a 26.2-mile marathon but a three-mile footrace up the towering Mount Marathon, which rises 3,022 feet from the ocean, and back. Runners are pitted against its slopes of forests, waterfalls, scree, snow, and cliffs. By anyone's standards, this is no ordinary race. It began as an argument in a bar between two sourdoughs in the early 1900s. The disagreement was whether the mountain could be climbed in less than an hour. A bet followed and a race was staged with the understanding that the loser would furnish drinks for the crowd. Local merchants got into the spirit of things by putting up a suit of clothes and other prizes for the winner. The race was staged for July 4.

The optimistic sourdough lost the bet; the winning runner finishing in one hour and two minutes. Since that time, Mount Marathon has been a long standing tradition in Alaska.

Mike Cragen & Troy after the 2001 Mount Marathon.

© Jenifer Trautwein

Next to the Iditarod, this is the World Series of sporting events in the Far North. Anchorage TV stations have live coverage on race day and 10,000 people stream into town to watch runners race up and down the mountain. Not only does weather challenge the competitors, but they also deal with snowfall still left on the mountain from the previous winter. Some years, the mountain is wet, slippery, and muddy, while other years, temperatures soar in the 80s, dehydrating and overheating runners. The record to date for the fastest finish, up and down, is 43 minutes and 23 seconds. That's an amazing time for the race, which begins and ends with a half-mile run through the streets of Seward.

UPDATE: Tragedy marred the 2012 race, where a 66-year-old first-time competitor went missing and was presumed dead, a 41-year-old runner suffered life-threatening injuries in a fall and a 34-year-old woman was seriously hurt after a fall.

Running this race seemed crazy. But on July 4, 2000, I found myself intrepidly standing at the starting line. This race has become so popular that officials now limit it to 300 men and 300 women. To even enter, runners literally camp out in the middle of winter in the local Chamber of Commerce's parking lot to vie for the few open spots that aren't filled by the previous year's entrants. A friend hoping to coax me into running the race volunteered to camp out and get me signed up.

I was no stranger to this mountain. I had hiked it countless times from various routes. More than once I've flown off the top in my paraglider – once even in the dead of winter on Christmas Eve. From the top, the views of Resurrection Bay and the National Park are second to none.

Most serious runners train for months – even years – for this race. I held no allusions of winning this race, so I did not train at all, feeling that if I "had" to train, I had no business being on the starting line. I keep in good shape and hoped to finish in the top 100 at least. My goal was to get up and down the mountain in at least 80 minutes.

The race begins with a mad sprint through town to the base of the hill. Before I even start climbing, my lungs feel

Reaching the top of Mount Marathon on race day, July 4.

© Ron Niebrugge/www.wildnatureimages.com

ready to explode. The trail up the mountain is steep and difficult, requiring heavy use of the cardiovascular system and extreme leg muscle exertion. Often I find myself on all fours, winded and climbing vertically up tree roots, dirt inclines, as well as rocky faces. With so many runners on the mountain, the trail is single file and I can only go as fast, or slow, as the person in front of me. It is very difficult to pass and keep a steady pace.

I march on and on and on, sweating and vowing the entire time that I would never run this race again. As I near the top, I can hear the firehouse siren sounding in the distance, announcing the arrival of the leader approaching the finish line. I am utterly dumbfounded. The winner is already up and down the mountain and I am not even to the top – the halfway point! I'm not in all that bad of shape, but I am astounded that someone could climb that quickly. (The winner finished in an amazing 45 minutes.)

As I crest the summit and begin the descent, I pass eight runners contemplating how to deal with the 300-foot snow chute before them. As a long-time mountaineer, I am at home on steep snow. I jump right in and begin sliding, just barely in control. The snow takes me about a quarter of the way down the mountain and the rest of the way involves navigating loose rock and scree. Quick and nimble feet are critical, as one misstep can mean hospital time (or worse).

The most difficult part of the descent comes at the very bottom of the mountain. Here you drop into a rocky chute complete with a cliff and waterfall. On tired leg muscles, a runner can have problems with this area. By taking my time I am able to navigate my way down without incident. However, the runner just in front of me keeps stumbling out of control and falling, scaring both of us. He topples partway down the cliff but continues on, bloodied, but not hurt badly enough to slow him down. Years of experience in the mountains has taught me that uncontrolled descents are typically not safe descents.

The last quarter-mile of road running is accompanied by hoots and hollers from the crowd, the welcome back to level ground that all runners receive. On shaky legs, I cross the finish line relieved that this race is finally over. Happy just to have finished, I couldn't believe I made it up and down in 62 minutes and finished 53rd.

Running Mount Marathon gave me an entirely new and unexpected perspective on the Fourth of July. I returned for Mount Marathon in 2001, placing 18th in 53:08, and in 2002 (29th in 56:26). In those years, trying to be more competitive, I found the race to be even more grueling than my inaugural race. After that, I quit racing to devote training time to other interests (paragliding and kitesurfing) and to avoid risking serious injury.

Ridge soaring on the Australian coast.

© Troy Henkels

CHAPTER FIVE

FLYING HIGH IN AUSTRALIA

By the time I reached 8,000 feet, my pulse stopped racing and I was fairly certain I wasn't going to die. Falling from the sky was no longer a reality. Altitude meant safety, and flying just below the clouds, I was safe.

In early December, I left the darkness and bone-chilling cold of an Alaskan winter to seek warmth, solitude, and some perspective. It was in Australia. My plan was to explore the country for eight weeks and do as much paragliding as weather would allow.

Paragliding is much like hangliding, but simpler and less gear-intensive. Hike up a mountain, lay out the wing, hook into the harness, run off the ridge, and fly like a bird.

Soaring at cloud base over Australia.   © Troy Henkels

Simple. As a boy, I had wildly vivid dreams of soaring over Mississippi River bluffs on hot summer days. Paragliding has made that dream a reality, and on lucky days one can not only soar, but also travel long distances riding thermals, much like hawks on lazy Midwest afternoons.

This trip to Australia was necessary. I had found myself slipping into the doldrums of a routine lifestyle that beckoned for some disruption. Working a 9-to-5 job near a large population base had taken its toll on my psyche, and it was time for a break. Craving solitude and a renewed perspective on how I wanted to live my life, two months of paragliding in Australia seemed like it might be a good start.

Matt, a fellow paraglider pilot and friend, accompanied me for part of the trip to seek out the best paragliding spots around Australia. We found the best flying in the small country town of Manilla in New South Wales. In the middle of summer in this part of the country, it is so hot that just sitting in the shade causes one to break out in a sweat. One of my journal entries reads: "The heat hits you like a wall and takes your breath away. There is no retreat until the late

hours, just before dawn." The sun and hot weather in Manilla produce great thermals for paragliding, so we decided to stay for several weeks. Just to fly.

Each day by 10 in the morning we were on the local hill named Mount Borah, waiting for the midday thermals to take over and carry us to higher, cooler altitudes. My best day paragliding in Manilla is impossible to forget. It turned out to be my best and worst flight ever. Just like every other day, despite the excessive heat, I dressed for cool weather. It was more important to stay warm if I was lucky enough to ride thermal lift to the coveted cloud base, where it was much cooler.

After setting up my wing and checking all the lines, I quickly launch into a thermal that pulls me off the ground and takes me straight up into the sky, just like smoke being sucked up a chimney. Within 15 seconds I am 100 feet above the launch point. Suddenly, with no warning, the fabric of my glider crumples up and collapses. Unknowingly, I had flown into solid turbulence that turned my wing into a useless piece of flailing fabric. As my wing oscillates wildly out of control above me, I begin to plummet back to Earth. The distance to the ground is so short there is no time to be scared, throw my reserve chute, or really even react. Within seconds of impacting the ground, and a certain end, my wing reinflates, corrects itself, and starts flying again. With my heart racing, I am barely able to fly away from the hill. The entire episode lasts less than 10 seconds, but it feels like an eternity. Matt watched the near-fatal accident from the ground and couldn't believe it. His emotions went from being horrified at what could have happened to relief as I flew away safely from the hill.

Although paragliding is an extremely safe sport, it does involve foot-launching a non-fixed wing aircraft. Consequently, the wing and pilot are at some mercy to the wind and atmospheric conditions. Accidents do happen.

When I am calm enough to start thinking again, all I can focus on is getting out of the sky and landing in one piece. Several minutes pass as I head out to the landing zone. I happen to fly through a big, smooth thermal that gently lifts me up. I turn and stay with the lift, circling its inner perimeter as I gain altitude. I begin thinking what a shame it would be to pass up such a nice thermal, despite my near-death experience minutes earlier. I keep circling, gaining altitude with each turn. In this sport, altitude is safety. With altitude, if something goes wrong there is plenty of time to react and hopefully sort it out by maneuvering or, if not, throwing the reserve chute. Earlier, this was not an option as I was too close to the ground for a reserve deployment to do any good.

This thermal takes me higher and higher and eventually tops out just below the clouds at 8,000 feet. I had gained over 6,000 feet of altitude. I fly with the wind, searching for another thermal, slowly losing altitude until catching another and climbing back up to cloud base. The conditions are perfect to soar for hours, and I was not the only one to enjoy it. At one point, an eagle lets me know I'm in his air space and he's not interested in sharing. He can easily thrash my wing with his talons. For 10 minutes he circles with me until I fly out of his territory. The search for thermals continues, and several times I lose the lift and sink slowly, searching for a landing zone and dreading the inevitable sweltering hike back to the road system. Somehow though, I always find a thermal that carries me back up to cooler temperatures and safer altitudes.

My perspective is constantly altered when looking down on the world from high above, perched below a lightweight piece of fabric. The Australian Outback is fascinating in its own right, but experiencing it in this way is an extraordinary experience. The landscape is so vast it's like a painting that absorbs you. It's easy to imagine the Serengeti in Africa to be like this; savannah, hot, dry, vast, quiet, and wild. It wouldn't surprise me to see a lion at any time, but of course I never do. The hardworking farmers and ranchers that survive in the area are some of the most warm-hearted people I've met anywhere and certainly are not far off from my roots in Iowa.

Finally, late in the day, after the sun had worked its way to the horizon, a pair of kangaroos watch as I softly touch down in a farmer's field. This turns out to be my best flight ever, having spent three hours in the air and traveling more than 40 miles across the Australian Outback. Later, reflecting on such an eventful flight, I realize that traveling just below the clouds, looking down from 8,000 feet on a summer day, in the middle of Australia, offered just the perspective and solitude I'd been searching for.

Loaded and ready to hit the trail, Iditasport 2000.   © Erin Rae Kittredge

CHAPTER SIX

BIKING IN PARADISE

Under a full moon, at 3 in the morning in the Alaskan bush, I began to wonder exactly where I was. I had been pedaling my bike for 18 hours straight and knew that I should be at the finish line of the 100-mile endurance race. Called the Iditasport because of its course around the famous Iditarod dogmushing trail, the race was fashioned much like the dog race, only for a much shorter distance. A simple idea really: a 100-mile race, human powered, with the entrant getting to pick his or her mode of travel. The choices are easy, considering the race takes place in the middle of winter. That aspect alone narrows the field to skiers, runners, snowshoers, and bikers. This is the biggest variable. If there happens to be several feet of fresh snow, the snowshoers have the advantage. If it is a dry winter and the trail has been hard-packed by snowmobilers, then the bikers have the easier going. This keeps the race interesting and it changes every year, and often times during the race, because any one discipline can have the advantage at any point in the race.

I had been procrastinating for weeks over the decision whether to enter. I was not interested in pushing my bike for 100 miles or enduring minus-40 degree temperatures, just for the "fun" of it. My preference was for perfect weather, hard trail, and easy pedaling, yet I knew it was rarely this way. Two days before the race, I paid my $300 entry fee and started to figure out how to fit the required 15 pounds of survival gear and food on my bike. Being in shape wasn't a real issue as I had done some serious six-mile training rides. After all, how much worse could 100 miles be than six? I was in good shape and reasoned it was all in a day's ride.

Before I know it, I find myself shivering at the starting line with more than 100 other semi-sane competitors, eager and anxious to tackle a long day in the Alaskan bush. Temperatures are in the high 20s and getting warmer with the sunrise. The forecast includes rain and snow. The first eight miles of the course traverse a series of lakes, and more than once I find myself sliding across the ice on my back, my bike out ahead of me. Being of the old school, I had not outfitted my bike with expensive, wide, studded tires. After the fourth time hitting the ice, I decide to slow down a bit until I am off the ice.

The next 25 miles are a treat to ride because the trail is well-traveled all winter by snowmobilers, and this hard-pack trail is suited for a mountain bike. Part of the thrill of doing this race is the opportunity to ride through a part of Alaska that I hadn't seen before. It is quite an experience to travel under your own power, in the heart of Alaska, in the middle of winter. The only thing I can liken it to is the excitement of exploring back roads in Iowa when I was 12 years old. Thoughts of those dusty roads are all I can think about to keep me going for the next 60-odd miles.

As the forecasters predicted, it begins to snow. Big, wet snowflakes cake my bike rims and brakes. They weigh a lot. It is so warm that, even dressed in my lightest long underwear, I am nearly overheating. The warm weather makes for miserable traveling for the next 20 miles. Oftentimes the snow is so slushy that I can't bike through it. Letting most of the air out of my tires, until they are nearly flat, allows some flotation through the slush – but often not enough. When I start pushing my bike, the real work begins, and I can only hope for rideable trail ahead.

At each checkpoint, spaced at intervals of 20 or 30 miles, I fill my water bottles and eat as much food as I can in less than 10 minutes. Although I have no hopes of finishing in the top 10, my competitive spirit pushes me to finish as well as possible.

By the halfway point, poor trail conditions so demoralize me that my thoughts constantly turn to never entering this race again. Although I feel good, I have to search for the motivation to continue. Much to my surprise, I learn there are several skiers still ahead of me. That is all the motivation I need. Now my goal is to catch them, even though the snow conditions favor skiers.

Soon afterward, bad trail conditions grow even worse. I fly over my handlebars several times while zooming downhill, and I realize that my front tire is sinking, axel-deep, into the soft snow before I can react. The front tire comes to an abrupt stop and violently throws me over the handlebars. This excitement lasts only a short time before I begin walking my bike down the hills, recognizing the imminent danger of injury this far into the race.

By sunset, my pace is back on schedule. I descend onto the Yetna River and temperatures plummet toward zero. Seemingly all of sudden, there are no trail makers anywhere to be found. Out of nowhere, there are eight other bikers, equally as lost on the ever-widening frozen river. Everyone has a theory of where the trail might be. The idea that makes the most sense is that we had somehow missed a trail turnoff and now are on the east shore of the river when we should be on the west. The consensus is that going downstream is the best bet and that eventually we will reconnect with the trail. Eventually, this turns out to be true, but not until we spend two hours and numerous extra miles pushing our bikes, often through knee-deep snow.

Getting back on the trail is uplifting, and I begin pedaling the last part of the course faster than I do the first half. My spirits soar as I head for the Little Susitna River and the final checkpoint, only 12 miles from the finish. If I maintain this pace I will finish by 3 in the morning and in good standing. However, it becomes difficult to ride very fast because I can only see as far as my headlamp will illuminate the trail. The temperature continues to fall. By 3 in the morning, I have yet to reach the last checkpoint. My odometer is showing nearly 100 miles, so I know I must be close. This just urges me on. I continue to follow the green trail markers that the race official repeatedly told us to follow. (This is the only race using green for trail markers.) Feeling the finish line is close, I pedal with a vengeance.

At mile 98 I hear an owl high in the trees and wonder how much more alive a person could feel, alone in the night in the middle of Alaska. Out of nowhere, I hear a snow machine behind me. I pull off the trail to let them pass. Oddly, the driver stops and I immediately ask if he knows where the finish line is. In low tones, he breaks the news to me. A dog sled race happens to be using the same trail markers, and I had made a wrong turn. I was nearly back to civilization – but 10 miles off course. Ten miles doesn't seem like much, but, after 18 hours on my bike, it is a long way. There is no way I can fathom the prospect of riding the 10 miles back, and then cover another 12 to the finish line. Physically exhausted and mentally drained from concentrating on the trail for so long, I am relieved to hear them say it is within race rules to accept a ride back to where I made the wrong turn. I could continue from there. Lucky for me, someone saw me make the wrong turn and informed officials. My pace must have been fast, because it took them almost two hours to catch me. I was lost and didn't even know it. The half-hour snowmachine ride back to the trail was more frightening than all other elements of the race – plus much colder.

Once back on the bike, there are still 12 miles to the finish. By this point, I am exhausted and any uphills are difficult work. I pedal on, enjoying the wilderness and the experience, yet remain firmly convinced that I will never enter this race again. Ever!

My drive to compete is long gone, and so are any close competitors. Without fanfare, at 6 in the morning, I cross the finish line and hobble inside to let race officials know. It takes me 21 hours and 18 minutes to finish. I am the 27th biker out of 61 bikers, and 30th overall out of 122 racers. Although exhausted by the finish, I feel it is a pretty good finish, all things considered. Unbelievably, three skiers finished ahead of me. The winner finished on a bike in 11 hours and 45 minutes. To date, I have never done the race again ... although every winter it does cross my mind.

After ordering a burger for the drive home, I loaded my bike onto my Subaru and drove home to sleep. It was possibly the best cheeseburger I have ever eaten.

CHAPTER SEVEN

THE MOOSE'S TOOTH

At 4 in the morning I stick my head out of the tent to check the weather. Clear, windy, and really cold. I hunker back down into my sleeping bag as the wind rattles the tent, and mumble to Seth, "Bluebird day." This means that the weather is perfect to attempt the mountain we had come to climb, the Moose's Tooth.

My infatuation with this Alaskan mountain started the first time I set eyes on it. A towering peak that rises with immense 4,000-foot vertical rock walls from the Ruth amphitheatre glacier basin, to the 10,335-foot summit. Although modest in comparison to its 20,320-foot neighbor, Denali, its topography is so convoluted it offers climbing challenges that are far more technical than any I had experienced in all my years of mountaineering in Alaska.

For years, my dilemma while thinking about climbing this peak was who to take as a partner. Seth, being only 23, had paid his dues and earned his experience in the mountains from the day he first came to Alaska as a 19-year-old. My trust in him was implicit and we had sharpened our skills on vertical terrain by ice climbing together all winter long.

The plan was to be dropped off by airplane as close to the

The view from base camp, Moose's Tooth.

© Troy Henkels

mountain as we could, ski to a base camp, and wait for good climbing weather. The route choice was simple. Most of this mountain is vertical rock, and, not being rock-climbers we had to find a weakness that would allow us access to the summit ridge. After extensive research, we settled on the west ridge. It's a spectacular route that ascends steep couloirs and several ice falls before giving way to the west summit. From there, we would traverse steep, heavily corniced ice pitches to the true summit, almost a mile away. Simple enough. Or so we thought.

For weeks leading up to the climb I had countless people ask me, "Why?" "Why do you climb?" "Why take risks?" "Why do you go to the mountains for refuge?" "Why must you get to the top?" My simple answer was, "Is there a better way to spend Easter?" Yet for years I have searched for a single answer to this often-asked question, and have found none. The best explanation I can offer is found in a mix of camaraderie among climbing partners and the embrace of nature, while exploring the outer limits of human potential.

Mountaineering is survival, self-sufficiency, and challenge, not only physically but mentally as well. There is a kind of trust and teamwork that I have found nowhere else in my life. For

The Moose's Tooth is just left of center with the summit hidden in a cloud. Our climbing route was up the snow slope on the left and along the ridge on the left skyline.
© Troy Henkels

me, it's a medicine for the mediocrity of everyday life. Time in the mountains and climbing have a way of putting one's life and existence in perspective, in very short order.

Tent-bound waiting out bad weather.   © Troy Henkels

The first 20 of our 24 hours of this trip, we listen to the nerve-shattering sound of avalanches rocketing down the mountains surrounding our base camp. With aching backs from being stranded in the tent due to bad weather, we reason that people go to the mountains to endure, for our biggest challenge to that point is one of patience. With more than a foot of snow having fallen since our arrival, our hopes of reaching the summit are looking dismal. There is no sign of perfect climbing weather in sight. We had estimated that our summit bid could take as long as 24 hours round trip, and we would need a large "good weather" window to succeed. Spending a night high on this peak is not a desirable option, possibly deadly, and not in the plan. Our wait continues.

After the third day, the weather breaks and it truly is a Bluebird Day – not a cloud in the sky. But the wind is relentless. Having shivered all night, we know it is well below freezing outside. The temperature inside our tent is a balmy 5 degrees Fahrenheit, so we know that venturing out in the wind is a cold and risky proposition. We wait for the sun and hope the wind will die down. With the sun comes ambition. We gear up and head out, into the wind, to climb the Moose's Tooth.

The first difficulty is getting across the glacier to the base of the icefall and couloir where we will begin our ascent. After successfully navigating a minefield of crevasses we savor the view of the Alaska Range on a rare clear day. Both of us know how lucky we are to have this good weather. Our

ascent of the couloir begins in knee-deep and often waist-deep snow. Climbing in these conditions is miserable and physically exhausting. Not only are we on a steep slope, but, next to us are the remnants of a recent avalanche from the icefall directly parallel to our route. Chunks of ice the size of large trucks litter the slope and wreak havoc on our nerves. If that isn't enough, a hanging glacier offers us precariously perched ice chunks some 800 feet directly above us. Seth and I realize the importance of spending as little time as possible in this couloir. The dangers are obvious. As a result of the exhausting conditions, we frequently switch off lead and the daunting task of breaking trail. As the slope steepens, the time spent in this dangerous couloir turns into hours. With Seth in lead and breaking trail, I suddenly hear and feel a large "whooomph!" from the snow below us. When I yell at Seth, asking what that is, he doesn't move. He catches his breath and says the whole world just fractured right under his feet. We both stand still and silent, knowing what that means. Avalanche! We were climbing on a huge slab of hard-packed snow that had an unstable layer of snow under it. This layer fractured under our weight, settled, and was ready to cut loose in an avalanche, wash us down the mountain, and bury us in the process. After a few moments, nothing slides, and we spring into action. Frantically, we climb higher and out of the danger zone, feeling extremely fortunate not to have been buried somewhere near the bottom of the icefall.

We anchor ourselves to the mountainside and discuss our options. We look skyward at the dizzying route and are certain that we can make it at least halfway up this mountain. After that, the ridge is extremely vertical, heavily loaded with snow, and quite dangerous. It would be suicide to go higher, and we know it. A retreat was prudent, despite the desperate

Starting up the climbing route.   © Troy Henkels

feelings of wanting to get up this peak. Part of being a good climber and staying alive is knowing when it is time to back away. We start our descent and travel in silence; we both know the climb is over. Our summit bid would have to wait for another year and for better conditions. Retreating the same slope we climbed is quick business when going downhill, and we manage to get back to base camp without further incident.

Despite our failure, Seth and I stayed in the mountains for three more days. Not to climb, but to experience the immensity and majesty of the Alaska Range in springtime. We ski-toured around the Ruth Glacier, riddled with crevasses hidden under deep snow, just so we could look up vertical rock walls soaring thousands of feet above us. For three more days, we relished in our dream, of life in the sun, cold, and fresh air in the mountains of Alaska. Some days you just know you are alive, and thankful for it.

Jeff King leaving the start chute in Anchorage, Iditarod 2009.

© Troy Henkels

CHAPTER EIGHT

RIDING WITH THE KING

When I moved to Alaska in the early 1990s, I became friends with a guy named Jeff King. I knew Jeff as the chief of the local fire department in Denali Park, where I was a volunteer. The first winter I knew him, he asked if I wanted to help with Iditarod. Without really knowing what I was getting into, I said yes. Little did I know that my friend, the fire chief, was also the Michael Jordan of the dog mushing world.

For Jeff, there is no greater experience than standing on the back of a dogsled, howling with the dogs at a full moon on a crisp night in the middle of the Alaskan wilderness. But there is so much more involved with dog mushing, particularly for a professional long distance sled dog race competitor. It's a lifestyle, an all-encompassing lifestyle. Over years of winning races, his front yard has been transformed into a state-of-the-art dog yard, housing 60 to 140 dogs and puppies at any given time. This is necessary to build dog teams of the caliber necessary to be one of the top mushers in the world. Having won the Iditarod four times, in addition to a long list of other race wins, Jeff King is considered the "winningest" musher in the world today.

Being friends with Jeff has allowed me the opportunity to experience a lot of what 140 dogs have to offer, as well as the excitement of spending time with an athlete at the top of his game. During one particularly cold December, I was

Jeff with Salem at Iditarod start 2010.   © Troy Henkels

visiting Jeff in Denali National Park. We loaded the dogs into their specially built boxes on the back of his pickup truck and headed out for a training run. Driving out the Denali Highway, we passed a sign that read: "Travel Beyond This Point NOT Recommended. If you must use this road, expect extreme cold and heavy snow. Carry cold weather survival gear. Tell someone where you are going." Roads in Alaska can be a bit sketchy, particularly in winter, but I had never traveled on one posted with such stiff warnings. As we zipped past the sign, I wondered what I had gotten myself into. For Jeff, it was just another day at the office.

Jeff regularly uses this long, lonely stretch of remote, snow-covered road near Denali Park to train his dogs. On this day we would alternate between riding the sled pulled by 10 or 12 dogs and driving the truck with the balance of the dogs hitched up to, and seemingly pulling, the truck. Both the sled and the truck are a means to keep the dogs going slow enough so they don't burn out. The goal is to train the dogs to run at a pace that they can maintain for 1,000 miles. The dogs love to run, and if left up to them, they would sprint hard and tire quickly. This exercise really is marathon training for canines.

Typically, with dog mushing there is never a dull moment. After several hours on the trail, with Jeff driving the truck and me on the sled, we see a dog team approaching.

47

Riding second sled with Lisa Frederic, Iditarod 2009.   © Maggie Kelly

There is a sled in tow but no driver. Jeff jumps out of the truck and onto the sled I'm driving. He tells me to jump on the oncoming sled when it comes by. Catching and stopping a 12-dog team is no small challenge. As the dogs zip by, I jump onto the sled, get them stopped and turned around. To the dogs' dismay, we head the direction they had come from. After about 20 minutes, we come across a friend training her team. She has never been happier to see anyone in her life. She is sweating and near exhaustion from running to try to catch her team. It turns out that when she had stopped to fix a harness, the excited dogs pulled the anchor out of the snow and made off down the trail before she could grab hold of the sled. As luck would have it, we came along and saved her from a very long day.

These marathon training runs are in preparation for the Iditarod Sled Dog Race, which has been taking place the first weekend of March for over 30 years. Mushers all over the world dream of running this race and, if they can find a way, it becomes their focus. The race starts in Anchorage, covers approximately 1,000 miles through the barren Alaskan landscape, and finishes in Nome. In the downtown streets, there is much fanfare, and race start day always proves to be an intense and interesting experience. There are cameras, interviews, sponsors, last-minute preparations and lots of hoopla. Mushers must contend with a circus atmosphere with 80 teams of 16 barking dogs each, and blocks of spectators standing shoulder-to-shoulder and cheering. In the midst of such excitement, it is easy to see why a team of humans is needed to assist each musher.

Since 1995, I have been a dog handler for Jeff on start day and, in some years, at the finish in Nome. There are last-minute preparations, packing, and repairs to be done for the team's driver but the race is really about the dogs as they are the star athletes in this marathon. Their health, safety, and care are of utmost importance to compete. The handler role is a simple, yet important one: Take care of the dogs and make sure they get to the starting line safely. When it is time to get on the trail, the dogs know it and their excitement is contagious. The adrenalin flows as we pull to hold lines taut and lead the team down the streets, lined with hundreds of barking dogs, to the start line. Once the team is off and running, the dogs settle into a steady pace and hunker down for 1,000 miles of racing. They leave the handlers behind.

===============

"FOUR – THREE – TWO – ONE – GO!" Twelve Alaskan huskies, harnessed to pull the required tandem sled configuration, break free from the starting line with overwhelming power. I am balanced on the narrow runners of the second sled. The cold wind stings my face as the team whizzes past the roaring crowd. When leaving the downtown starting point of the ceremonial start of the race, mushers are required to attach a second sled behind the first, for safety reasons. The second sled and driver adds weight and an extra hand if there is a tangle somewhere along the winding streets of Anchorage.

That 20-mile ride lasted several hours – hours that I will never forget. A second team of Jeff's young dogs, known as a "B" team, is driven in the race by our friend Lisa. This is the ultimate training run to prepare the young, inexperienced dogs for the next year's competition. Lisa allows me the opportunity to drive the second sled for her. It is the closest I will come to feeling what it is like to embark on a 1,000 mile journey to Nome behind a team of dogs. The support and encouragement from spectators is nothing short of astounding. That day I learned if you are a dog musher in the Iditarod, you are a rock star.

Jeff on the trail, Denali Park, Alaska.   © Troy Henkels

Jeff has won the Iditarod four times (1993, 1996, 1998 and 2006) and holds the distinction of being the oldest musher to ever win the Iditarod (age 50, 2006). We remain close friends and most recently began exploring the Alaska wilderness in other ways.....with motorcycles and small pack rafts.

Jeff and I share a similar fascination and love for the Alaska wilderness. Jeff's enthusiasm for the state and his unconventional lifestyle as a dog musher have always inspired me to chase my dreams and continue to explore around life's next corner.

Chevron.   © Troy Henkels

Standing at the South Pole, 1996.

CHAPTER NINE

AROUND THE WORLD ON NEW YEAR'S EVE

© Troy Henkels

The turning of the New Year always reminds me of my most memorable New Year's Eve. Two months into a five-month stay in Antarctica, working at a U.S. research station in McMurdo Sound, I was sent to the South Pole to repair a piece of equipment. My excitement could barely be contained when I boarded the nearly 30-year-old, ski-equipped C130 military aircraft for the three-hour flight due south. The beat of the engines and smell of exhaust was in stark contrast to the pristine white environment that was framed by the plane window. I was going to the South Pole!

My senses are overwhelmed as I peer out the window at the Trans-Antarctic mountains. The expansive ice fields, towering unclimbed peaks, and glaciers that go on forever are like nothing I have ever seen. The three hours pass, and when the C130's skis touch down on the polar plateau, I am bursting with excitement. Stepping off the plane I am blinded by sunlight reflecting off the snow and ice. The intense cold alarms me as I search for something to cover my face. This is going to take some getting used to. As far as the eye can see is the flattest and most desolate landscape that I have ever encountered. The geodesic dome that serves as the research station's base has a mysterious feel to it. This is where my work begins, in what would turn out to be a month-long stay.

Throughout my time at the Pole there were a lot of rumors about activities that supposedly took place on New Year's Eve. No one talked about any specifics, only that I should be at the geographic pole on the 31st at midnight. This was important because in Antarctica there are actually three poles. One is the magnetic pole, many hundred miles away from the South Pole station. A second is the ceremonial South Pole, where everyone gets their pictures taken. It is marked by a candy-striped pole with a mirrored ball on top and surrounded by the flags of all the nations that have

signed the Antarctic Treaty. The third is the geographic pole. This is marked by a stake with a brass marker on top stating the location to be 90 degrees south. This is the exact location of the South Pole. Nearby is a sign with quotes by explorers Roald Amundsen and Robert Falcon Scott, whose expeditions were first to reach the pole (1911-12).

The rare opportunity to even experience Amundsen-Scott South Pole station is special, much less to be there to ring in a new year. For the next three weeks, I carry out my job duties, anxiously anticipating the holidays at the Pole. Outside of work, there are a few interesting diversions that only take place at the South Pole. On Christmas Day, there is a footrace called "Race around the World." This involves running three laps around the C130 skiway and thus, three trips around the world. With the wind chill, it was minus-65 degrees Fahrenheit, and runners were checked each lap for frostbite. Finishing in fifth place was good enough for me, especially considering the conditions. The other diversion, also on Christmas, is to place a ham radio call to my parents in Dubuque. My Mom and Dad are surprised and happy to hear from me and they send their well-wishes to the bottom of the world. While I enjoy a quiet holiday under the stations geodesic dome, I imagine a very different holiday season back home.

Everyone works on December 31, and there is very little talk of any festivities. However, someone does mention that the actual South Pole marker has to be moved each year. Because the South Pole sits on top of a two-mile-thick ice sheet, and the land beneath is an angled slope, gravity is pulling the ice off the underlying topography at a rate of 30 feet a year, downhill toward the Weddell Sea. At the current rate, the South Pole will be under water in 140,000 years! So, each year, the geographic pole marker must be moved 30 feet. And this supposedly happens each year at midnight on New Year's Eve. With no one getting prepared, I am beginning to have my doubts.

At 20 minutes before midnight, I begin dressing in three layers of fleece, down parka, hats, gloves, neck gator and all the other necessary extreme cold-weather gear. This takes longer than expected, and as a result I am late. With burning

Reflections at the South Pole.   © Troy Henkels

lungs from the cold air, I sprint to the Pole in hopes of not missing anything. But no one is there. I look at my watch, and it is still six minutes until midnight. At four minutes to the hour, the party begins to arrive. First comes a group with champagne, followed by a group singing, and then the guy with the new pole marker and a tape measure. He quickly measures 30 feet and, precisely at midnight, proceeds to pound in the new geographic South Pole marker. Everyone cheers, drinks, hugs, dances and kisses. Each takes a turn at pounding in the new South Pole marker: a unique way of making history and starting off the New Year. Oddly enough, the sun shines brighter than ever at this party in the middle of the night at the bottom of the world. As the parties break off to go their separate ways, there is talk of ringing in the New Year, each hour for each time zone, as the world rotates. Some people just take it all in and enjoy the moment a little longer, lingering in the bright sunshine of the frigid night. My celebration starts when I take out my boomerang and throw it around the world, not once, but several times. This was certain to be one of those once-in-a-lifetime opportunities. With the wind biting my cheeks, I catch my boomerang and smile, knowing this is a moment I will never forget.

Photo left: Exploring the Imax crevasse
with the Search and Rescue Team.
© Troy Henkels

The seemingly endless Polar Plateau, Antarctica.
© Troy Henkels

Ski equipped C-130 taxiing for takeoff at the South Pole.

© *Troy Henkels*

CHAPTER TEN

LIVING SIMPLY IN SIPLE DOME

After three days of dreadful weather, the plane lifted off the polar plateau and headed north. It is the only direction to go from here. It was just another plane ride, yet it was not one I would soon forget. After spending nearly a week at the South Pole, I was going home, back to the U.S. research station McMurdo on the coast of Antarctica. In the middle of my second assignment as a Communications Technician, this time around would be a 12-month stay. The three-day weather delay was welcome. It allowed me more time to be overwhelmed by the South Pole: the vast, flat, wasteland of ice and snow in all its splendor. For a thousand miles in every direction is a landscape so expansive, desolate, and cold, that it remains largely unexplored even today.

We take off for McMurdo, some 800 miles away. The three-hour flight was stunning when I flew to the Pole, and I knew it would be equally enthralling on way back. Looking out the window of the cargo hold and cockpit, I remain mesmerized by a landscape composed of so many shades of white and a chaotic symmetry of snow, ice, and mountains that stretch to the horizon.

This day is special, as the pilots decide to fly low through the Trans-Antarctic Mountains, which span the continent and remain virtually unexplored. Our plane flies so low that, instead of looking down at mountain peaks, I am looking up at them. The deep crevasses of the Beardmore Glacier, many times wider than our plane, is an overwhelming sight. From the cockpit I watch as we descend from the mountains into a fog bank that engulfs McMurdo and the Ross Ice Shelf. As I take my seat in the cargo hold, the pilot slowly climbs above the fog. A short time later, we learn that the weather in McMurdo had turned bad and we could not land. This is a problem: We do not have enough fuel to return to the South Pole. Antarctica is known for its rapidly changing weather. It can deteriorate without notice. That is the case on this day. Because there are few places for us to land and refuel, it is anyone's guess where we are

headed. This is Antarctica, after all.

As the plane makes a sharp bank east, we fly past Mount Erebus, the only active volcano in the Antarctic. Before long, the pilots tell us we are heading to a remote, deep field camp on the Ross Ice Shelf. It's called Downstream Bravo. With this diversion, and after four hours of flying, we will be only one hour closer to McMurdo than when we left the Pole. As could be expected, everyone on board is nervous and apprehensive about this unplanned rerouting.

We land at Downstream Bravo, a flat, white frozen plain, at the same time uninspiring yet impressive as the South Pole. On the horizon is a trace of mountains while the sun casts an eerie pinkish, orange glow through the thick overcast skies. Downstream Bravo consists of only two Jameswarys (small military Quonset hut tent structures) and several windbreak walls built out of snow blocks. There is an outhouse, very little food, and no space for 26 people to sleep. We are welcome to use the windbreaks to brew some hot chocolate. This camp is usually occupied by two people and used not only as a fuel stop, but also for minor research on gravity, altitude, glaciology, and magnetism. It is a remarkable yet dismal place to be stranded.

Once inside the main Jamesway, I remain fixated to the radio as the pilots talk with McMurdo, South Pole, and Siple Dome, another deep field camp. Our options for the night are: Refuel and go back to the South Pole, which now was a four-hour flight; stay at Downstream Bravo, which would require camping outside on the ice shelf. (Some in our party are already building igloos, just in case); or fly to Siple Dome, a larger field camp that could accommodate everyone. The decision is Siple Dome. This field camp has food and beds for all of us for as long as we are stranded, which in Antarctica could easily be days or even weeks.

Nobody really knows what to expect, as Siple Dome had been the talk around McMurdo for several weeks. No flights had been able to land for over a month there due to the severe weather. In total, there had been 40 cancelled flights, and the Siple residents had not seen fresh fruit, vegetables, mail or new faces for a very long time. Because of this, many are concerned we would land at Siple and not get out any time soon. Unlike everyone else, I anticipate being stranded.

After refueling, we take off, travel another hour across the ice shelf, and land at Siple Dome. In the murky overcast weather, this place looks just like Downstream Bravo – a flat white, lonely expanse for as far as you could see. Siple Dome is the largest summer field camp ever deployed by the U.S. Antarctic Program. There are up to 60 residents and 12 Jamesways. The ice at Siple is about 3,000 feet thick and ideal for studying coastal climate conditions. This area also offers climatology information dating back 100,000 years, so it is a place of great scientific interest.

Already after 6 in the evening, the Siple crew had dinner waiting for us in the galley. Our flight was the talk of the town, as we were the first new faces anyone had seen in quite some time. A celebratory buzz filled the air, not to mention a birthday to celebrate, as well as a disco party scheduled. It strikes me as extremely peculiar that a remote Antarctic outpost would host a disco party. Unreal. After dinner, it is confirmed that we will spend the night and hope for clearing conditions in McMurdo by morning.

This information holds little relevance for me. I am already out the door with a set of skis and a large traction kite. The wind is perfect as I unfurl my kite. A fog bank rolls across the ice and engulfs the entire area. Another guy from Fairbanks, Alaska, is a kite flyer, too, and he fetches his gear. We strap on skis and are soon zipping through three inches of fresh snow at about 25 miles per hour. It is an intense feeling and a bit unnerving to be sailing through the fog with no real reference to the ground. The sky and ground are white on white with no real differentiation. Because of the fog, sound travels very well, yet it was challenging to stay within a close proximity of town without getting hopelessly disoriented. We would get several miles from town and follow the wind and our tracks back from where we started.

After several hours, exhausted, I kite-ski to where I would stay: a cozy Jamesway hut called Valhalla, about a mile from the main camp. It's the only Jamesway not in the main town area.

I pull up and see two of my South Pole friends soaking in hot tubs of water … OUTSIDE! I am out of my gear and into the water in less than two minutes. The crew at Siple Dome knows how to live AND survive in comfort, despite the harsh Antarctic conditions. They had hooked up a water heater and a circulating pump to three circular tubs that looked like horse troughs. There is music blaring from a jambox somewhere in the background and the water is hot and feeling great. We talk, laugh, and make strange shapes out of our freezing hair. Visibility is nil, and that adds to the overall magical feel of this experience. After an hour we retire to a small wooden building nearby. It's a sauna!! Same routine as the hot tub, and it is bliss.

Finally, it is time to check out the disco party. We drive our snowmobiles into town and find the party in full swing. There is loud music and even louder dancing. I am a little too tired and relaxed from a long day of flying planes, kites, and hot-tubbing to get into the swing of the party. Just as I am about to leave, we learn that two more scheduled flights from McMurdo are cancelled. That makes the total 42. Cheers go up from the crowd, and the tally is recorded on a board labeled, "Joke of the Day."

By now it is 2 a.m., and I retreat to a cot for a few hours of sleep. In another world, in another time and place, flight delays would mean something very different. In the Antarctic, it means the rare opportunity to live simply, out on the edge of an ice shelf.

By 6 a.m. the next morning, everyone is up and back in the galley, waiting on news about the weather in McMurdo. Oddly enough, the fog has cleared and we are off the ground by 7:30. The return flight to McMurdo is uneventful. Everyone is asleep or trying to sleep. As we work our way across the Ross Ice Shelf, I remain glued to the window, taking in the view of Mount Erebus, Mount Terror, Ross Island, the Weddell Sea, the Royal Society Mountain Range, and McMurdo itself. These are views I will never forget.

I have mixed emotions as we finally touch down on the ice runway at McMurdo. As I step off the plane, it dawns on me that sometimes its not just flight diversions and delays, but life's diversion and delays that turn out to be the unforgettable experiences. This is one of them.

Solstice alpenglow over Mount Fellows and Pyramid Peak, Denali National Park.   © *Troy Henkels*

CHAPTER ELEVEN

SOLSTICE

Over the years, summer solstice, June 21, has come to mean a lot of things to me. As a boy growing up in Northeast Iowa, it was the long semi-lazy hot days of summer spent pulling weeds in my father's melon patch and mowing grass in the apple orchard. Daylight well into the evenings found me riding country roads on my bike, just to see what was beyond the next hill. In those days, it was my curiosity that kept me exploring.

As life became busy with school and, eventually, work, solstice carried less meaning for me. Marathon study sessions and interminable work days provided little notice or opportunity to appreciate those long days of summer.

These were misspent days, caught up in what many people call "real life." Days spent being too busy to really notice and enjoy the small incremental changes of sun and seasons. One always knows what season it is, but the subtle changes often slip by when bogged down by the responsibilities and time constraints of a life in society as we have come to know it.

Before long, after two years at a traditional job, I was looking beyond that next hill of my life, and without realizing it at the time, looking for some meaning in solstice again. I quit, I moved, I left that life and made a life in which I could be happy. A life full of rolling hills that beckoned me for exploration and adventure. I went north to Alaska.

59

Early winter light from Black Island looking at
L-R: Mount Erebus, Mount Terra Nova, and Mount Terror

High above the Dry Valleys, Antarctica.   © Dan Bryan

Exploring the Ross Ice Shelf with the Search and Rescue team.

© Troy Henkels

June 21st, 1998. Midwinter polar plunge at Scott Base. Water temperature 29F, air temperature 0F, with a stiff breeze. I'm only in for 15 seconds.

© Dave Smith

In the northern latitudes, I found a new meaning in summer solstice. In Alaska, people savor that day and celebrate it. Back in Iowa, summer solstice meant 15 hours of daylight. In interior Alaska that means 22 hours of daylight. My days and light-filled nights were spent exploring every hill and mountain I could. I recall 14-hour hikes across mountain ridges, watching the sun work across the northern sky just dipping below the horizon before rising again. Through sun, rain, and snow I hiked on, mystified by the small changes around me.

Another solstice found me looking even farther north. I pointed my car that direction and drove until I could go no farther. The end of the road is Deadhorse, Alaska, and the Arctic Ocean. Here it is truly an endless summer solstice day. It never gets dark.

Other solstices found me deep in the Alaska range, navigating streams, glaciers, and other dangers in an effort to climb high peaks. The extended days were welcome. They allowed climbing at night, when the snow and ice are colder and less apt to avalanche or collapse into a waiting crevasse. More than one solstice was spent on mountain peaks watching the sun circle the sky in an endless display of light, as it decorated the clouds a myriad of colors. A few years ago, I spent the solstice on a mountain, waiting the perfect conditions to fly. Just before midnight, I launched my paraglider in a smooth southerly breeze and cherished the moment as I drifted to the valley floor far below.

As a result of these days spent up north, summer solstice has come to hold special meaning to me and is treated much like a holiday. I'm always searching for a way to make each summer solstice a day to remember. Little did I know, in the summer days of my youth and the summer nights in Alaska, that the solstice of 1998 would be different.

This particular solstice found me deep in the midst of an Antarctic winter: 24-hour darkness. No sun. No sign of any sunlight. When I signed a contract to work in McMurdo for 12 months, I never considered summer solstice – or midwinter day, as it's called in Antarctica. The logistics and planning for a year there were enough to distill any thoughts of what a year on the ice would hold, much less solstice. Even the first six months on the ice found me basking in the 24-hour daylight of an Antarctic summer. Days were spent with my job duties and all the activities that go along with life on the ice. Never did I suspect what this solstice would hold – a variety of things, things that are surprising to me even now, as I write this.

That winter solstice found me playing in a rock band at McMurdo Station. Purely for fun and the entertainment

Performing in the southernmost rock band in the world, July 4, 1998, McMurdo Station, Antarctica.

© Troy Henkels

of the 166 winter-over staff members. Even during my days playing in high school rock bands did I imagine such a destiny. The long days of darkness found me out on the Ross Ice Shelf with fellow members of the Search and Rescue team, practicing for possible emergency scenarios. Climbing ice, jumping from crevasses, and rescue pulley systems all take on new meaning in the dark and cold of yet another solstice.

Most notably, there was the annual polar plunge with our New Zealand neighbors at Scott Base. They were kind enough to chainsaw a hole in the sea ice for the pleasure of all to take a dip into the 29 degree water. When I climbed out of the water during this solstice, I knew it would be one that I could never duplicate. Such a bizarre combination of darkness, water, cold, ice, stars, and bare skin. Afterwards, a cup of warm cocoa and a long ski across the ice with no destination in mind. Just the stars, the moon, and solitude. As I begin to wonder what next year's solstice will bring, I'm aware that summer solstice has taken on new meaning in the long, dark Antarctic winter.

CHAPTER TWELVE

DUELING WITH DENALI

Part 1

Life gets interesting sometimes, or so I thought, when I agreed to a climbing expedition on North America's highest peak, Denali – commonly referred to as Mount McKinley. Little did I know at the time how interesting my life would get. My partner, Ford, a 52-year-old Denali veteran, had first attempted this peak 25 years earlier – meaning that I was only 7 years old when he made his first attempt. He had been dreaming of reaching the summit for longer than I had been alive. Ford had climbed big peaks all over the world, but Denali had defeated him on three attempts. When I first considered this expedition, it seemed like a small undertaking, as I was in the middle of an Antarctic winter and somehow, I wrongly presumed that a climb up Denali would be a cakewalk compared to spending a winter in the Antarctic.

Sorting gear in preparation for climbing Denali.   © John Cantalupo

Many months were spent organizing the expedition and working out logistics to insure we were prepared with ample food and gear to survive whatever Denali could throw at us. Our timeline was to spend 25 days on the mountain. If we couldn't reach the top in that much time, well, then it was not meant to be. Most people don't realize that 25 days might not be enough on a mountain that creates its own weather. It could have ambient summer temperatures in the neighborhood of minus-30 and minus-40 degrees Fahrenheit. Denali is home to some of the world's most dangerous glaciers and awe-inspiring mountains. At 20,320 feet, Denali has been compared to many Himalayan peaks because of its high latitude and extreme rise from sea level to summit. It has the most dramatic vertical rise in the world, greater than even Mount Everest. As a result, Denali experiences some of the world's most severe storms and gets the full force of weather moving inland off the Bering Sea and North Pacific. In the short Alaskan climbing season, which runs from late April to early July, Denali can see as many as 1,000 climbers. Success rates vary, but typically are no better than 50 percent due to high winds, cold temperatures, poor weather, fatigue, accidents, frostbite, and altitude sickness.

Having lived in and around Denali Park for many years, I had plenty of time to dream about reaching the summit. It's hard not to think about climbing a mountain that dominates the landscape the way Denali does. In those years, I paid my dues and acquired mountaineering skills, climbing smaller peaks all over the Alaska Range. With my apprenticeship complete, it was time to set my sights on bigger tasks in the mountains. We decided a two-person team was best, with no guide, and up a well-known route, the West Buttress.

Denali from Talkeetna, Alaska.

Several days before we departed for Talkeetna, the jumping-off point to fly into base camp, Ford looked at me and said, "We'll see dead people up there. I have every trip." This I knew was a very real possibility – and even understood that it could be one of us. It made me wonder about the sense of climbing a peak where there is the inherent risk of not coming back alive. For me, mountaineering is a calculated risk, and it is always dangerous. Climbing big mountains and living on glacial terrain has allowed me some of the most difficult, yet rewarding experiences I have ever had. Death and injury happened to "others." Ford's statement made me realize this isn't always the case. He would be leaving a wife and three children behind for this climb, while I, on the other hand, was leaving behind my trusty 1983 Subaru.

Denali base camp at 7,200 feet on the Kahiltna Glacier.

© Troy Henkels

Part 2

On May 18, we drive to Talkeetna. The weather is beautiful, and we take in remarkable views of the mountain we hope to climb. In a state that can have more rainy summer days than sunny ones, we felt the clear weather was a good omen. Once in Talkeetna, we spend several hours sorting out hundreds of pounds of gear and food. This is a job in itself, as is packing the ski-equipped bush plane with everything that we will need to live for 25 days on the mountain.

In less than an hour, we go from spring in Alaska to winter in the Alaska range. The flight over stunning mountain passes and enormous glaciers goes quickly, and we land at base camp on the Kahiltna Glacier at an elevation of 7,200 feet. Shortly thereafter, we watch a high-altitude Llama helicopter arrive in camp unexpectedly. It is attempting to rescue three Brits stuck in a terrible storm near the summit. Two are rescued in the highest helicopter extraction in history. It will be two more days before they find the third guy – cold but alive. He will lose both arms and legs due to exposure and frostbite. This, at the onset of my climb, really makes me wonder what I am doing here.

Our plan is to climb expedition-style, which really means climbing the mountain twice. We will carry loads of supplies up the mountain, cache (stockpile and bury) them, and retreat to our lower camp. The next day, we will move camp up to where we have cached our gear. At this rate, climbing Denali is a long and tedious endeavor. Not only is this necessary to shuttle loads of gear, but it allows climbers' bodies time to adapt to the high altitude.

Roped up and ready to climb on the Kahiltna.

© Ford Reeves

Our first eight days on Denali are perfect. Almost uncharacteristically, the weather is clear, sunny, and at times even hot. Being too hot and dehydrated is more of a problem than being too cold. The temperature at night is below zero but daytime temperatures soar above 60 degrees. The days of covering miles and miles on the gradual slopes of the glacier seem endless. Although not technically difficult, days traveling on the glacier are hot and exhausting.

By the fourth day, the terrain begins to change. Our world is becoming more vertical. We camp at the base of monster hills with names like Ski Hill, Motorcycle Hill, and the headwall. It seems that every day the hills get a little steeper, the air a little thinner, and the weather a little colder. By Day 9, we are dug in at an elevation of 14,200 feet; our accommodations look more like an artillery installment than a campsite. We build four- to six-foot walls all around the tent to protect our temporary home from Denali's infamous high winds and extreme storms – something we have yet to experience.

On the 10th day, the weather changes dramatically. A low-pressure system moves in, bringing overcast skies and storms. No one is moving up or down the mountain. Despite this, we still feel the need to position our supplies higher up the mountain to ensure the best chance of success if the weather does break. We decide to carry gear and food up the headwall to 16,500 feet. With calm, overcast skies and light snow, the three-hour trip up turns out to be fantastic. For safety's sake, because of the severity of this slope, the top portion of the headwall is protected with fixed ropes and anchors. We make full use of our front-pointing crampons on the 65- degree ice; they are a must on this wall.

This is the first day that I feel like we are actually climbing. Before we reach the fixed ropes on the most dangerous section, we encounter four groups, all descending and complaining of extremely dangerous conditions higher on the wall, including extreme cold and with wind gusts of up to 60 miles per hour. Despite their warnings, we continue. We are two hours into the headwall and determined to cache our 50-pound loads at the top of the wall.

This is the kind of climbing I enjoy, and I really feel in my element on this wall. We battle freezing fingers and climb on for another hour and a half to the top of the wall. Protected from the wind by a large rock, we talk with a small group of Belgians who had just completed the same climb. They are as excited about the weather as I am. They plan to continue onto high camp at 17,200 feet, which, in this weather, appears to us to be suicide.

After burying our supplies, we carefully find our way to the top of the fixed lines and descend back to our camp at 14,200 feet. By the time we return, the wind has calmed down a bit, but it is still overcast and snowing. We feel lucky to have pulled off getting our supplies stashed, despite the questionable weather. However, we still face the dilemma of how long we would wait for the weather to break before attempting to move higher.

Part 3

The camp at 14,200 feet is the staging area for climbers. There are as many as 40 people in camp, so we are in fine company. We make good friends while stuck here due to the bad weather. It becomes quite interesting watching the group dynamics play out, as teams struggled against the mountain. Daily, we watch a young team from Quebec battle to get up the mountain, only to return exhausted at the end of the day. There is a very strong pair from Wyoming that makes a summit bid after spending three miserable days at 17,200 feet. They turn back halfway to the summit in 60 mile-per-hour winds and with frozen fingers.

And there are the Lander Boys, three National Outdoor Leadership School instructors from Lander, Wyoming, with an aversion to laughing, singing, and having fun. They are the best friends we are to make on Denali. With our best wishes,

they head out to move to high camp in less-than-desirable weather. Five hours later, after exhausting themselves on the headwall, they return. One of their members is experiencing cerebral edema, swelling of the brain. Because edema can result in rapid death, they retreat back to 14,200-foot camp. A very strong team from Fairbanks waits out the bad weather for only two days at 14,200 feet and then retreats at the first news of an unfavorable weather forecast for the next four days. We meet people from all over the world while waiting out weather at 14,200 feet. There are Spaniards, Polish, Canadians, Argentineans, Norwegians, Russians, Italians, French, Romanians, Germans, British, and even one climber from Basque. Exchanging stories with climbers from all over the world is a major highlight of this climb. No one cares what your job is or how much money you make. Everyone is here to climb, and that is all that really matters.

After eight days in camp at 14,200 feet, our patience is wearing thin. We see teams move higher in hopes of good weather and return defeated. Sitting in camp, waiting, is the most mentally and emotionally demanding part of the climb. In a world of thin, cold air, human defenses break down quickly, and our team is no different. Without a favorable forecast in sight, we even start discussing the possibility of abandoning the climb. We both know that every day spent on the mountain is making us weaker, physically and mentally. Before it is over, each of us will lose 10 pounds.

Finally, on Day 17, we awake to clear, calm, sunny skies. We quickly melt enough snow to supply us with water and pack up our camp. The long climb this day will take us to 17,200 feet and our high camp. We climb the headwall in unbearable heat with heavy loads, only to reach the top and have to pick up our cache and more weight. Climbing at this altitude with an 80-pound pack is not even remotely enjoyable. Above the headwall, the terrain gets a bit more difficult. The route follows a rocky spine ridge and becomes very technical, with dropoffs exceeding 3,000 feet. A trip, fall, stumble – or any error at all – will prove detrimental and possibly fatal. Fortunately, we navigate this part of the route flawlessly and arrive at high camp safe but thoroughly exhausted.

That neither of us feels altitude sickness is a positive sign that we had spent ample time acclimating at lower elevations. Setting up camp, however, is a job in itself. Trying to find the

Photo left: Climbing above the headwall, headed to 17,200 feet.
© Troy Henkels

motivation to cut blocks of snow to protect our tent is a chore. All I can do is one task – and then sit and rest for a while before I can do more. At this altitude, even in the middle of the day, it is extremely cold. Rest breaks are short. Fortunately, there is no wind. After several hours, camp is set up, snow is melted, and food is prepared.

The night is spent recovering from the brutal climb and discussing our game plan. We hope for another clear day, but Ford is unsure if he can climb 3,000 feet on back-to-back days. I have no idea if I can either, but I am willing to try if we have the weather to do it. We decide to get up early and climb higher as long as the weather looks good. My experience in the Alaska Range taught me to climb in good weather whenever it is available.

Part 4

We awaken to clear, sunny skies and no wind. The ambient air temperature is minus-20 degrees Fahrenheit. One of our biggest concerns is not the cold temperatures as much as the wind. It had been an extremely windy season on Denali, even though to this point we have experienced very little of it. We pack light loads consisting of food, water, and a few extra clothes. Roped up, we head across a basin to yet another steep hill leading up to a landmark called Denali Pass. In the shadow of the mountain, this section of the climb takes nearly two hours and is extremely cold. Just trying to keep our fingers from freezing requires us to stop and warm them up every few minutes. When we crest the top of Denali Pass, I am relieved to finally be in the relative warmth of the sun. However, when I feel a 10-knot wind coming up from the other side of the pass, I realize things would be getting even colder.

With both of us feeling well, we keep climbing. My presumption that the top of Denali Pass is about halfway to the summit is terribly wrong. I realize this six hours later. We slowly but steadily climb higher, into the rarefied air, and struggle with each step to get enough oxygen into our systems. At this point in the climb, the terrain is not dangerous, except for the possibility of crevasses. With very few breaks, we climb for hours, hoping to utilize this window of good weather. We take a short break below the last long steep hill leading to the summit ridge. Immediately,

Traversing the summit ridge.

I sit down and drift into a deep sleep. I have never been so physically and emotionally exhausted. Before climbing Denali, I read about climbers on Everest that sit down exhausted, unable to climb on. They become hypothermic and freeze to death. With an oxygen-depleted brain, I drift into sleep, hoping that no one will wake me and I can just stay where I am – and die. As long as I don't have to climb the next hill, I am OK with that. Thankfully, Ford awakens me to continue on. Before long, we pass the Lander Boys on their return from the summit. Emotions run wild as we hug and cheer their success. They give us fair warning of the terrain ahead and how far we still have to go. We press on.

Attacking the last steep face requires slow, steady steps, and many rest breaks. It is a demoralizing, near vertical face that stands between us and our goal. At several points during

72

© Troy Henkels

the ascent of this face, I find myself at the edge of my physical and emotional capacities. I break down in tears. Denali has taken its toll on me and it is still demanding more.

When the realization hits me that, indeed, we will make the summit, that brings on tears as well. After an hour, I pull myself over the small cornice at the top of the face, and look down 6,000 feet to the glacier below. I sit down to get my bearings – before I have time to stumble and take a deadly fall. I belay Ford up, and we take in the immense views and analyze the summit ridge. This narrow knife-edge ridge is shoulder-width and leads all the way to the summit. We discuss protecting the ridge with oversized stakes, called pickets, but opt to save time and go without. We know that one slip could be our last, so making a mistake is not an option.

On the summit with a picket (anchor) that my Dad custom built.

© Ford Reeves

The last ridge to the summit is long and arduous. Time after time, we encounter false summits. My adrenaline is in overdrive as I lead across one of the wildest ridges I have ever been on. In the thin air, we climb higher across dangerous cornices and drop-offs of several thousand feet in each direction. Finally, we reach the summit of Denali. I am standing on the top of North America.

I belay Ford up. And then we share a moment of tears. It has been a long journey, and it has taken more effort than either of us had anticipated. Yet we both know the journey is only half over.

Part 5

We take in the immense views and savor the Alaska Range in all its beauty. No one knows better than Ford that it might be a while before either of us would stand in this special place again. He waited 25 years for this moment to stand on this coveted mountaintop. For 15 minutes we endure the minus-25 degree ambient temperature and 10-mile-per-hour wind. We look down the ridge. It is time to retreat to our camp at 17,200 feet. It has already been a long day, and we still have many hours of descent before reaching the relative safety of our tent.

Both of us know that most accidents on these expeditions happen on the descent. That's when exhaustion, fatigue, wind, and bitter cold take their greatest toll. However, our descent of the summit ridge, and the steep wall leading up to it, is flawless. Once back on the wide expanse known as the football field, it seems weird to me that I can hardly walk. Every time we stop, I fall over, unable to stand.

As Ford leads us, little does he know the condition of the man on the other end of the rope. I stagger downhill like a drunkard. I can't control my legs. My concerns grow. We still had to navigate a long, difficult descent. I yell to Ford to call for a rest break, fall to the ground in confusion, but then resume the sporadic pace I am creating. I do this repeatedly. To compound our difficulties, the wind has picked up, making it colder and creating greater problems with visibility. We can deal with the weather, but my lack of leg coordination is perplexing.

As I stagger and stumble, my mind races. What would happen if I am unable to descend Denali Pass? It's due to the thin air, I'm sure, but it takes me hours for my brain to figure out what is wrong.

Part 6

At the top of Denali Pass we take a break. I have to. Finally, it dawns on me: My body does not have sufficient fuel for what I am asking it to do. Because of the wind and cold, I have not eaten all day, and I have had only half a quart of water over the past 10 hours – not nearly enough. Something has to change before I attempt the dangerous slopes of Denali Pass, or this will be a fatal trip down. I eat and drink as much as I can, and I begin to feel better. Coordination and strength return to my legs, and we continue down the pass. Both of us know that this is a critical part of the descent, especially when we are battling fatigue and the cold. Fortunately, we make it to the glacier below without incident.

The traverse across the glacier back to our tent is a miserable experience. The wind has picked up to 40 mph and a ground blizzard is blotting out visibility. The safety of our tent is within reach, and we know that we will make it, but now our concern is for the teams we had passed coming down, those still heading toward the summit. It is late in the day and, considering the deteriorating weather, they will have a difficult time getting back to camp without having to bivouac high on the mountain. This could be a fatal situation. One guided group and a team from Michigan still remained high on Denali.

After 11½ hours, we crawl back into the tent. We had done it. We stood on the summit of Denali, something both of us had dreamed about for many years.

Ford, exhausted from the climb, falls asleep immediately. I feel great, thanks to the food and water consumed at Denali Pass. I stay awake, boil water, and cook food. A while later, I awaken Ford to eat and drink. We need to be fueled to continue our descent the next day.

A few hours after our arrival in camp, the Michigan team shows up, battered and cold but in good spirits. They had reached the summit and returned without incident. It wasn't until the next morning that we learned the guided group had

Retreating back to camp after hauling a load of supplies to 14,200 feet. © Troy Henkels

Ford, happy to be back © Troy Henkels
at camp after a long day
reaching the summit.

summited, but did not make it back to camp until midnight, in the peak of the storm. All members suffered frostbite of some degree on their faces, hands, and feet, but thankfully no case was severe enough to necessitate a high-altitude rescue.

Part 7

By morning, the wind is gone and it is clear. After packing up camp, our descent takes us on the same route we had come up two days earlier. Our loads are obscenely cumbersome and heavy. We slog down some of the most diverse, beautiful terrain in the world. Above the headwall, we pick up what is left of our cache, making our loads over 100 pounds. This makes the headwall extremely difficult and, without the wind, a sweltering sun does not help matters at all. The irony on Denali is that it seems to either be too hot or too cold, and for our descent down the headwall it was too hot.

Once at 14,200-foot camp, we pick up another cache and try to eliminate any weight that we can. We jettison all our extra food and fuel. Fortunately, some groups ascending have underestimated their needs and are able to use our extra supplies. Some Russian climbers take all our food; several minutes later, they show up with a huge skillet of scrambled eggs with ham. All we can understand them saying is, "We make American breakfast for you." We are more than grateful, as this breakfast fuels us for the next 12 hours as we

make our way back to the safety of base camp.

We load our packs and sleds and continue down the mountain under sunny, clear skies. We hope to get off the mountain before the next storm moves in and leaves us stranded. Thoughts of cheeseburgers and summer keep us moving, despite our worn-out bodies and minds. By midnight, we are safely back in base camp and enjoying the Moose stew that we had cached 20 days earlier. Quite possibly, it is one of the best meals I have ever devoured.

Part 8

The next day, under sunny skies, we wait for our bush pilot to fly us back to Talkeetna. After spending 20 days, standing atop the summit, and keeping all appendages intact, Ford and I are proud and happy. As other teams battle the heat of mid-day, we are on our way back home to summer, friends, and family. We feel good.

We watch an older man struggle into camp. Sporting a plaid flannel shirt and multi-pocketed fishing vest, we recognize him from our summit day. We pepper him with questions. Through his broken English, we learn that he is 60 years old and from Poland. He has not climbed in 15 years, lives in the U.S. and is a professor at Louisiana State University. His wife believed this climb was a suicide mission, and she returned to Poland to be with family when

Heading back to base camp on the Kahiltna Glacier.

© Troy Henkels

Back in Talkeetna after a successful climb. © *Troy Henkels*

As we wait, another man skis into camp under some distress. He tells Annie, the base camp manager, who directs all the flight operations, that he had made the summit and his partner, who would be along in about an hour, "has a bad leg." We learn from Annie that this second man, the one with the "bad leg," is Ed Hommer. But the description is not exactly true. He doesn't have a bad leg – he has no legs. Ed was the first double amputee with prosthetic legs to summit the highest peak in North America.

Years earlier, Ed's bush plane had crashed at Kahiltna Pass and a rescue was delayed for several days because of bad weather, during which time frostbite claimed both his legs. He had returned, climbing the mountain that caused him to lose his legs. This was Ed's second attempt in as many years. This time, he reached the summit and was in great spirits. Ford and I are impressed beyond words. Feeling very humbled, we load the plane and leave the mountain, thus ending our expedition. We are happy to have summited, and honored to have met two men in a small place in time, that had accomplished exactly what we had, but under much more severe hardships.

Climbing Denali was more of an experience than I had ever dreamed it would be. Once again, I thought about how life certainly gets interesting sometimes.

she received news of his death on this great mountain. The longer we listen to this man, the more humbled we become. He had just soloed Denali, an amazing challenge in itself. Not only did this 60-year-old solo the mountain, he did it in eight days! After thinking summiting in 20 days is something to be proud of, we are astounded. The hour we spend talking with this guy is a pleasure, and we hold him in high regard. This climb is not rejuvenating his interest in climbing, but it is closing the book, the final chapter of his climbing career. This last hoorah is a splendid one. After listening to his theories of climbing and climbers, his voice still resonates with me, when he says, "So many nice places, why

Postscript: Years later, I crossed paths again with Ed Hommer – in an indirect way. Ed was killed by rock fall on Mount Rainier in 2002 when he was training for his second attempt on Mount Everest. In 2003, at base camp on Mount Everest, I met famed climber Jim Wickwire, who was on the other end of the rope when Ed died. Jim had come to climb Everest on the same expedition for which Ed had been training, and he would climb the mountain in his honor.

Ed back in base camp after standing on the summit. © *Troy Henkels*

Denali from Wonder Lake, Denali Park, Alaska.
© Troy Henkels

The Aconcagua massif from the air.

CHAPTER THIRTEEN

ANDES DREAMS

© Troy Henkels

Part 1

Despite news reports of rioting and killing in the streets of Argentina, I departed the darkness and brutal cold of an Alaskan winter for a summer climb in South America. It was a well-planned expedition, with promise of success and reaching the summit. Ford, my expedition partner from a successful climb on Denali several years earlier, would meet me deep in Argentina, on the edge of the Andes, to make an attempt on a big peak named Aconcagua.

This mountain towers over the scorched, arid landscape scaling to 22,800 feet. We figured that if we had success on North America's highest peak, it would prove to be a good recipe on South America's highest peak as well. Although this mountain is higher than Denali, it experiences much warmer temperatures and stronger winds due to its proximity to the Equator.

After months of planning, organizing, and packing, I was finally ready to go. For several weeks, however, our focus had shifted from the complexities and logistics of the climb to the turmoil and violence unfolding within Argentina's borders. There were 22 dead and 200 injuries. The president had resigned without a solution to the unrest. Instead of talking about "when we go," it became a question of, "Will we go?" My fear was that we were perfect targets. Seemingly wealthy Americans with flashy climbing gear would look like a good target for the 18 percent of Argentineans who were unemployed and countless more who were hungry. With any great adventure, there is a certain amount of risk, but this was just a dimension that we hadn't anticipated – yet it was one that could easily thwart our plans and put us in danger.

The trip to Argentina involved four layovers and 20 hours in the air. When I arrived, the sweltering heat and

At the beginning of the climb, Aconcagua towers in the distance.

blazing sun shocked me. Our jumping-off point was the town of Mendoza. News reports said the rioting had not been as severe in this town as in Buenos Aires. Never once feeling threatened, I explored parks and boardwalks throughout the city. People were happy and friendly, and you would never guess that there was high unemployment and civil unrest. The country had four presidents in as many days, and the Argentine Peso was being devalued against the American dollar. Overnight, prices on everything went up 40 percent, without an increase in wages. I couldn't help but wonder: What it would be like if this happened in the United States? Despite all this, we enjoyed the time because it would be the last civilization we would see for at least three weeks.

Part 2

Several wonderful days are spent in Mendoza sorting gear, waiting on lost luggage, and securing the required climbing permits. We depart under sunny skies and drive deep into the Andes. In all my travels I had never experienced mountains quite like the Andes. Every shade of red, orange, and brown in a myriad of symmetry, riddle these mountains, while the valleys below are green, lush, and full of life.

As our bus climbs, I know we are close to our departure point at 8,500 feet – a small place called Los Puquios, which translates to "warm spring." It is here that we hire mules to haul the bulk of our gear to Camp II and the point where we really start climbing.

We spend one last night in the lowlands, out of the sun, gearing up mentally and physically. The next day, by sunrise, the gauchos are gone, driving the heavily loaded mules with our gear higher up the mountain. These beasts of burden are impressive, hauling heavy loads to great altitudes every other day. It will be three days and 4,000 feet more before we will see our gear that traveled by mule. On our backs, we carry everything we need for the 20-mile trek into base camp. Under incessant sun and ever-present wind, I can't figure out if I am too cold or too hot. One minute I feel on the edge of heat exhaustion and the next, a blast of wind from high up would hit me and send me searching for warmth behind Gore-Tex and fleece.

Near a small kettle pond and a meadow of wild flowers, Ford and I manage one glimpse of the mountain we had come to climb; it's snow-covered and towers 14,300 feet above us. It is so far off in the distance that it is hard to imagine being able to hike to the base of this peak, much less getting to the top.

We feel good and manage the hike up 2,000 feet of breathtaking river valley, with monstrous peaks all around, in about two hours. Our camping spot is called Confluencia, because it sits in a pretty area where two mud-filled rivers meet and roar past in continuous thunder. Fortunately, Confluencia has a freshwater spring, which provides a much-needed commodity when going to altitude while temperatures soar into the 90s.

In this environment and far above tree line, there is no place to hide from the sweltering sun. We had sent our only

tent with the mules, so we would sleep under the stars and be subjected to the sun all day. Only small bits of shade are found under an overhanging rock. Originally, we planned to only spend one night at this camp, but the park rangers recommend two, for proper acclimatization to the altitude. We agree, but we brought food for only one night, so we are on half-rations already – the very first day of the climb! We aren't starving just yet, but we are feeling awfully hungry.

After a day in the blazing sun, we sleep in the clear and chilly night. The southern sky is chock full of stars, with no man-made lights to obscure them. What a special experience to gaze up at this sky in the shadow of spectacular peaks. The next day, we meet several other climbing parties coming down the mountain, unsuccessful in their bids to reach the summit. They report horrible conditions higher up: Three feet of fresh snow on the summit and seven feet at base camp. It is unthinkable to climb through seven feet of snow, so we aren't sure what to expect.

Hiking into Plaza Francia, trying to acclimate before continuing on to base camp.

© Ford Reeves

Battling heat and altitude, we climb 2,000 feet to a place called Plaza Francia, a spectacular valley offering stunning views of the formidable south face of the mountain with its huge and convoluted rock walls scattered with equally appalling vertical ice and hanging glaciers. Taking in this sight, I am at a loss to even find a route up this side of the mountain. It all looks too dangerous. I am dumbfounded, aware that numerous parties had scratched their way to the top via the south face. We spend the day high in this valley, acclimating, before returning to Confluencia for more half-rations and a night in freezing temperatures.

Early the next morning, we are on the trail to base camp, racing the sun and soaking up as much shade as we can before the sun torches our valley. Fortunately, it has been dry, so the rivers we have to cross are running low. We hike on. Heavily loaded mules can be seen coming up the valley in the distance, dust scattering to the wind.

After five hours, the trail starts to get much steeper. Our heavy loads and heat of the day take their toll. Two more hours, and we are up against an extremely steep rock face. As the altitude wears us down, we trudge on, knowing that we must climb this hill. We pass loaded mules coming down the trail. It is unthinkable that mules can negotiate this steep terrain – and several mule corpses lay below the trail, a testament to the severity of a fall.

Several climbers straddling mules pass us. Looking exhausted and ill, they are undoubtedly suffering from severe altitude sickness. It can be fatal if you do not descend in time. They are wrapped from head to toe to combat the sun and wind, and I can't help but wonder how they handled the blistering heat. With an eight-hour ride ahead of them, no one speaks. Certainly, these climbers are suffering from some miscalculation of human or natural error. Mountaineering involves inherent risks, and good climbers learn to calculate that risk and pursue their dreams in as safe a fashion as possible. But when dealing with high altitude, sun, wind, snow, and ice, there is always the unknown; risks can become uncontrollable. Most climbers believe they are exempt from such a fate, but no one is.

Part 3

After 8½ hours of grueling effort, we arrive at Plaza de Mulas/Camp II. This will serve as base camp to begin our assault on Aconcagua. Ford and I are exhausted from the heat and the altitude (13,890 feet). However, I am not prepared for what greets me at base camp. There, in the distance, is a hotel complete with running water and a restaurant! Near our campsite are large tents with signs advertising cold beer, Coke, cheeseburgers, email service, and telephones.

I had earlier read an article that described Plaza de Mulas as a "freak show," and indeed it is. This seemingly benign environment attracts people from all over the world who come to be guided up the highest peak in the Americas. Many are not climbers or have ever set foot on a mountain. There is a group of older Asians, trekking in on mules, in dress clothes. Another man is in dress slacks and a button-down shirt, as if he has just arrived from the office. There are many others who lack the gear, knowledge, and experience to attempt an assault on a peak of this magnitude. This explains the climbers leaving the mountain on mules.

We eventually learn to ignore the "freak show," but it leaves me wondering what scaling the world's highest peaks has become. Aconcagua, like Everest, has turned into a trendy place to climb. Just having the money and willpower to make it this far does not make you a climber. As a result, just like on Everest, people die. It's the sad reality when you mix big mountains with big money.

Part 4

Still adjusting to the altitude, we labor to set up camp on the scree field of glacial debris that would be home for the next 15 days. By nightfall, the temperatures plunge and we are resting in the warmth of the tent. We spend two glorious days at Plaza de Mulas, acclimating to the elevation change. It is a necessity if we are to continue higher and make an attempt at the summit.

Both days are warm, sunny, and windy. My time is spent sorting food and gear and figuring out what will be needed at

Late afternoon light on Aconcagua.
© Troy Henkels

certain locations as we moved higher. An immense amount of time is spent cooking and filtering the glacier water that we use to cook and drink. And, as with all climbs on popular mountains, there is socializing. This camp has more than 100 tents and at least that number of people. Climbers have come from all over the world and from all walks of life, united in the common goal of getting up this formidable peak.

Ford and I become friends with two 6-foot-6 brothers from Holland. They keep us laughing hysterically with their good humor on the complexities and difficulties of being tall and a wide variety of other topics. We also meet a man from the East Coast who has walked the Appalachian Trail solo; he is here to attempt this peak alone. He peppers us with questions because this is the first mountain he would ever climb. All the while, we look skyward at the route up the mountain. It doesn't look dangerous, but it has a huge, steep hillside of rock and scree that seems endless. Any climbers near the top are not even visible.

By Day 3 at Plaza de Mulas, we are feeling acclimated and anxious to move. We decide to take a load of gear to a higher camp. In high-altitude mountaineering, the philosophy is to climb high and sleep low. This means during the day you haul equipment to a higher altitude and return to sleep at a lower camp, allowing ample time for your body to adjust to the gain in altitude. Typically, after that, one can move camp to that higher altitude and feel somewhat adjusted to the higher elevation. We planned to do just that.

Part 5

Under sunny skies, we start our day loaded with gear, which will be cached 3,000 feet higher, at a camp called Nido de Condores. Having to climb a massive hillside is heartbreaking at this altitude. Although not technically difficult, the route switchbacks upwards for miles. Despite the inherent difficulties of carrying loads at high altitude, I am feeling good – really good. My pace is steady and strong, and I feel as if I can go on for days.

Finally, we are on the mountain itself, climbing, and making progress toward our goal, the summit. In the heat and wind, Ford and I both slog on, taking in the immense views as we gain altitude. Hour after hour, we climb, take a break, talk, and climb some more.

I reach a spot above a very large boulder, near where we would cache our loads, sit down, and wait for Ford. He is only 10 minutes behind me. But he doesn't show up. Is this a defining moment of the climb? I quickly run scenarios through my head of what could have happened. My fear is that he is sick or hurt. It is such a broad hillside that there is a slight chance he could have passed me without my knowing. I decide to climb for 10 more minutes, look around and cache my load at a place called Camp Alaska, at 17,100 feet. When I arrive, Ford is still nowhere to be found.

Suddenly I feel exhausted. Without realizing it, I had over-exerted myself and had not fueled my body with enough liquids or food. Now I am laying on the side of the mountain in pain. I have "hit the wall." Unable to walk, I am in agony, curled up with my head feeling that it is about to explode. I wonder if I can make it back to camp. I have climbed to altitude before, and I should have known better. Common sense finally kicks in, and I begin refueling my body with all the water and food I had left. After 10 minutes, I feel fine and begin a rapid descent, back toward base camp, in search of my partner.

Scouring the face of the mountain, I find no sign of Ford. After an hour and a half, I reach camp. And there is Ford, relaxing in the tent. He is in good spirits. It turns out that, just below the boulder where I had stopped, Ford decided to descend. We were no more than 50 feet apart, unable to see or hear each other due to the wind and steepness of the slope. Experiencing some internal struggles and just not feeling good about the climb, Ford had retreated to camp.

Fortunately, I have the utmost respect for Ford and understand what goes on while climbing, so I can't be upset. Mountaineering is as much a mental battle as it is a physical one. With a lot of things working against you (altitude, lack of sleep, physical exertion, etc.) it is easy to let the mental side of the game get the better of you. A good mountaineer knows their limits and when it's prudent to turn back. Ford did just that. Many times in the mountains, not recognizing this can lead to accidents or death, especially on big peaks like Aconcagua.

Part 6

As a result of Ford's retreat, we still need to have gear and food higher on the mountain, and we decide to make another haul the next day. This would help us acclimate and would still keep us on schedule. After almost eight hours of climbing, I am exhausted, so we retire for the day.

The next day, Ford decides he is not committed to the climb anymore, and it is time to go home. This is a disappointing blow, but I understand. I have been there. In the mountains, when you turn that corner and decide you'd rather be somewhere else, there is no point in going higher. To continue climbing only intensifies the recipe for an accident. Ford suggests that I continue the climb without him. Having spent enough time in the mountains with friends, I knew that decisions like these can impact a friendship for life, so this isn't even a consideration. I had come to South America to climb with Ford, not alone. The bottom line is that my friendship with Ford is more important than reaching the summit of Aconcagua.

However, I still need to retrieve some of my gear from higher on the mountain. I set out at noon under a baking sun and climb the same route I had traveled the previous day. After three hours, I pass my cache and continue on to Camp III, Nido de Condores, at 17,600 feet. It is a grueling, long climb, but it offers views across the Andes that are not visible from down low. After snapping a few pictures of the route to the summit, for future reference, I descend, pick up my load and continue down to camp.

Before sunrise, we pack up and head down the trail. We face a long day of hiking the Horcones Valley to the trailhead. We are surprised that the valley had changed. Rain lower on the mountain had turned everything green, and flowers are in full bloom. This welcome sight nearly overloads our altitude-drained senses. By nightfall, we are back in the town of Mendoza, feasting on Argentinean steak.

Camp 3, Nido de Condores at 17,600 feet.   © Troy Henkels

Part 7

Later, we learned that no one made it to the summit. All our friends had tried to reach the top, but a few days after we left, the weather turned dismal and it got cold and snowy. It snowed six feet at Camp III. The weather remained lousy for almost two weeks. Climbers managed to get to Camp III, where they waited for a good weather window. After an eight-day wait, most were so battered and exhausted that they retreated and went home. So, in retrospect, had we stayed, it is likely we would not have made it any farther up the mountain than we did.

Perhaps Ford had some internal insight that neither of us expected or anticipated. Most expeditions can't be considered a success or failure based only on reaching the summit. For both of us, it was the camaraderie and journey along the way that made our climb a success. Like many times in life, it's not about reaching the summit that is the important part. This I found to be true, at 17,000 feet on Aconcagua, deep in the Andes of South America.

The Southern most city in the world, Ushuaia, Argentina.

CHAPTER FOURTEEN

TRAVELING TO THE ENDS OF THE EARTH

© Laurent Dick/www.sailantarctica.com

Part 1

After our climb on Aconcagua, Ford and I landed in what I believed to be the southernmost city in the world, Punta Arenas, Chile. We were set to explore the wilds of Patagonia and the peaks of the Chilean Andes before flying back home. We had no itinerary and no real plan, strictly traveling by the seat of our pants, if you will. It felt good to be on the road again, and even better with no set itinerary. It seems the older I get, the more planned life and travels become, so this journey to South America was much anticipated. Patagonia was a place I had always dreamed of and only remotely ever expected to explore.

The day we arrived, I had asked Ford what he thought we might find to do in southern Chile. He said, "Well, we could go to Ushuaia." My immediate response was, "Yes, let's go there." I didn't even know where Ushuaia was. I had not even heard that word before. But I did know that, most times in life, not knowing where you are going ends up being an interesting experience. Ford explained that Ushuaia was really the southernmost city in the world and was reached with a variety of difficulties, many of which neither of us were aware of at the time.

By our third hour in Punta Arenas, we had had enough. This small city gave us a lasting impression of what life in deep southern Chile is really like. Everything had a cold and dreary feel to it – the architecture, the weather, the people, everything. It is not surprising for a place that sits at the very southern tip of Chile and is buffeted by constant winds and weather stumbling in from the Atlantic, the Pacific, and Antarctica. There seems to be no reprieve from the harsh elements, particularly the wind. Almost everything reflects that, even the trees that grow leaning with the wind.

Lake Pehoe and Torres del Paine, Patagonia, Chile

Part 2

We hit the road in a small rental car that we were assured is durable enough to withstand anything Patagonian roads could offer. We have to drive north and east in order to catch the only highway that will take us any farther south than we already were. About that time, I begin wondering what was at the end of that road. Did it just end at the tip of Cape Horn? We don't know, but we hope so, and are hell-bent on finding out. As we move across endless plains of rolling windswept bush country, the incessant wind blows in from the west across vast, deep blue lakes and the Pacific Ocean.

We come across the abandoned Estancia San Gregoria, a huge abandoned estate that resembled a ghost town of sorts, complete with the rusting skeletal hulls of a few large ships discarded in the 1940s, after a half-century of service. The place gives us a sense of loneliness, and it provides a solid reality check of how far away from civilization we are. And we stand to get farther away.

After several hours, we encounter a road like no other. It has always been my belief that, as Robert Waller once wrote, one good road is enough, but this takes that idea to the limit. In an attempt to save money, the government has only paved half the road. One side is pavement and the other is gravel. It puts us in a quandary: Which side should we drive on? Certainly, the pavement offered better driving conditions, and we soon learned this was the accepted protocol: Drive on the pavement no matter which direction you are traveling. If you are going the wrong way, then swerve into the gravel lane when an oncoming vehicle approaches. This proves for some excitement when traveling 60 miles per hour on blind corners. Eventually, the pavement ends, and it is all gravel. The gravel is so rough that we end up just driving in the ditch for quite some time. Yes, driving in the ditch was smoother and easier than driving on the gravel road.

The road finally veers south and we race to make the deadline to catch a ferry across the Straits of Magellan. We make it, just in time, and drive onto the ferry with a potpourri of vehicles destined for ranches and small establishments at various points farther south. The wind is relentless as we make the quick passage. The Straits of Magellan had been one of those mystical places that I had always heard of, yet never imagined crossing. Now I am here and it feels good. I wonder what it must have been like in 1520 when Magellan first passed through these straits. Somehow, in this part of the world, I suspect not much has changed.

Part 3

Back on the road, we travel for hours as the uninhabited landscape rolls past. We see the Atlantic and Pacific oceans in the course of a few hours of driving. Are there any other places on earth where you can actually do this? Late in the day we must pass through customs and immigrations, as Ushuaia is actually in Argentina, on a small strip of land that is somewhat removed from the mainland.

We pass through the Chilean version of customs and then, a few miles farther, the Argentinean version. Both are similarly staffed with unfriendly, armed military personnel who are excruciatingly slow. All procedures at both stations are manual. Five people at each crossing must look through our paperwork, each with a specific job which we cannot figure out. They look through our passports and stamp them. Ask a few questions, fill out multiple carbon copy forms that get signed by numerous different people. And, they punch our name and passport number into an ancient computer. Amazingly, it takes two people to do this, one to punch the keys and the other to show the operator where the keys are. Then, like everywhere in this part of the world, we are manually entered into a huge ledger. Ford and I are continually amazed at the inefficiency and labor intensive way things operate here. The entire time, no one speaks and we remain unsure if we'll be allowed into Argentina or out of Chile. We spend hours getting through both border stations, but at least we make it through.

Part 4

By nightfall we arrive in Ushuaia, the end of the earth. It is a much larger town than I expected, with an inviting cold feel to it. The houses are very industrial looking with a small area of town geared toward the small tourism industry that thrives for part of the year. We walk along the ocean and among shops in the middle of town, getting a feel for what life is really like in such a desolate place. Like everywhere in this part of the world, there is wind, and the landscape, people, and buildings reflect that. I'm intrigued by the solitude and remoteness of such a place and decide to visit this part of the world again, and stay for a while.

Ushuaia is surrounded by staggering peaks and sits right on the ocean. I'm reminded of some places in Alaska that occupy a similar setting. Amazingly, 43,000 people live in Ushuaia, a town that is wedged between the ocean and 4,500-foot peaks.

After a few hours, Ford and I drive out of town and spend the night by a small stream, where the fly-fishing looks promising and the stars explode across the southern sky. The next morning, we continue down the road until it eventually ends. Here we are: at the end of the road, at the end of the earth. We are in Tierra del Fuego, a National Park of sorts that encompasses a large land mass at the very southern tip of this continent.

We spend the afternoon taking in this beautiful place. We walk a half-mile from the end of the road to the ocean and look out, imagining that Cape Horn is not far off. A sign here informs us that we are at the end of the road and that we are 11,090 miles (17,848 kilometers) from Alaska!

For me, life is good when I can experience the extreme latitudes and visit places that I never knew existed, but am inexplicably tied to the place that I now call home. The landscape and mountains here remind me of Alaska, but the feel is different. The best I can suggest is to visit both places and you'll know what I mean.

Ford and I spend the day hiking and exploring the mountains, ocean, and nearby lakes. This place holds immense beauty and we want to soak up as much of it as we can, in the short time we are here. Fortunately we are far away from just about everything in the world, so there are very few people around. Just how we like it. After several days, we drive back toward Chile to explore points farther north.

Part 5

We end up logging thousands of miles exploring the far southern reaches of Argentina, Chile, and Patagonia. On the return trip to civilization our rental car breaks down, and we spend hours improvising a solution for repairs with nothing more than fencing wire, lumber, roadside rocks, and multi-tool pliers. With success, we limp into the next town for repairs with smiles on our faces. Early on, we had concluded that there are certainly worse things than being broken down in the middle of Patagonia with no tools.

A week later we are home. Looking back on that trip, I now realize that sometimes, the days that take you into the unknown and to places that you didn't even know existed turn out to be the most rewarding and memorable days in your life. So, if you wake up one day and someone suggests going to Ushuaia, just say "yes." You won't regret it.

Postscript: I did return to Ushuaia, in 2007. On that trip, I was fortunate to be able to spend more than a month exploring the city and surrounding mountains and ocean. I still maintain that if the opportunity arises, just say "yes" and go to Ushuaia. You'll be glad you did.

End of the road Tierra del Fuego,
17,848 kilometers (11,090 miles) from Alaska.

© Ford Reeves

L-R: Darran Wells, Sam Gehring, Troy, Elisabeth Gilbert, Mike Wolfert in Moab with Moab Global Extremes team.

© *Outdoor Life Network*

CHAPTER FIFTEEN

IT'S NOT REAL, IT'S REALITY TV!

Part 1: A Longshot

It started at a family reunion, on a hot summer day in Farley, Iowa, where my brother-in-law told me about "Global Extremes," an adventure-based reality TV show. Producers were looking for applicants to compete in a five-month, around-the-world adventure racing odyssey that would culminate with five finalists climbing Mount Everest. I had seen few reality shows that intrigued me, so I was only mildly interested. Figuring if it was TV, there would be a lot of people involved, and I didn't have much chance of making the cut. Nonetheless, I labored through the lengthy and detailed application process online and promptly forgot about it.

A week later, a "Global Extremes" producer phoned me with some preliminary questions. A week after that, I received an email inviting me to the first round of competition in Moab, Utah, a month later. Excited by the prospect of a winter traveling the world, having all sorts of wild adventures, I still didn't think something like this could really happen to me. It couldn't be real.

Out of 800 applicants, only 50 had been selected for the first round in Moab. After that, 24 would advance to a second round in Aspen a month later. Then, 12 would be selected to travel the world for three months, taking part in multi-sport races. From those 12, five would be selected to climb Everest. The 50 people in Moab read like a who's who of adventure racing. There were Eco-Challenge racers, marathoners, Iron men, and hard-core distance racers of all types. My experience in these type of races was minimal, and I began to question why I had been selected. My adventure resume was filled with cold-weather expeditions of endurance and unconventional sports, like paragliding and ice climbing. There was very little racing in my background, except for

a few backcountry races through the Alaskan bush, and the Turkey Trot in Dubuque, Iowa, on Thanksgiving 1979. Looking at the field of competitors, I thought it was obvious I could not compete with athletes of this caliber. So I decided to just show up in Moab, which features world-class venues for mountain biking and rock climbing, and have fun.

Five experts served as judges for the weekend and evaluated each person on a variety of attributes ranging from endurance, performance, attitude, determination, motivation, teamwork, and compatibility. We would be required to perform individually and in teams through a variety of activities throughout the weekend.

Part 2: Slow and Steady

Under overcast skies, we are split up into teams of five and run a multisport adventure course, several hours long, that requires the teams to work together. Right off the starting line, we have to swim across the Colorado River – a chilly prospect in October. Interestingly enough, not everyone can swim, and teams are evaluated on how they deal with this. Fortunately, everyone on my team is easy going and very strong. We fly through the course, which includes crossing the river four times, running through the desert for miles on end, and solving minor rock-climbing problems.

Day 2 finds us displaying individual skills higher in the mountains, starting with rock climbing. With a range of climbs to choose from, people can easily find something they could get up and show off some skills. However, what makes this interesting is the weather – the temperature is right at freezing and snow fills the air. This is quite challenging, even for experienced rock climbers, who must deal with numb fingers and wet, cold rock.

Moab, Utah.   © Troy Henkels

Next, on mountain bikes, we ride through six inches of mud mixed with snow on an epic downhill ride that takes nearly five hours. In that much mud – and to the delight of the TV camera operators – hardly anyone can keep his or her bike upright. By nightfall, we are all cold, wet, hungry, and covered in mud. It is becoming more apparent who might be eliminated from the competition.

Each day is progressively harder, and by Day 4 we are told there would be a biking and running race over a mountain pass at an elevation of 10,000 feet. It will start with a 15-mile bike ride, all uphill, followed by a 12-mile run, four miles of that uphill. I have no illusions that I will make the cut with this crew, so I decide to just maintain a steady pace throughout the race and see where I end up.

The start is a sprint, and I am amazed how fast people in front of me seemingly disappear. There is no way I can keep that pace; I don't even try. But, after a few miles, my steady pace starts to pay off, and I begin to pass people who bolted from the starting line like jackrabbits. By the transition from bikes to running, the race has slowed considerably, and I am able to pass quite a few more people. As we gain elevation, the snow becomes deeper; when we reach the top of the

pass, it is knee-deep. Fresh snow from an overnight storm has slowed the pace even more. I am able to pass a few more people on the way up. If I'm good at anything, it is running down mountains. I pass even more people on the way down. I'm surprised to finish in eighth place.

Gathered around a bonfire that night, the group is bursting with anticipation. The judges express their difficulty in choosing only 24 athletes from such a talented group of individuals. When the names roll, I am one of them! In a month, I will travel to the Elk Mountains in Aspen, Colorado, for Round 2. Mystified at making the cut, I return to Alaska wondering what I have gotten into.

I knew very little about adventure racing, so I call a close friend who is an ex-Navy Seal, marathoner, and adventure racer. His advice is to just show up, be yourself, and have fun. He knows I am in good enough shape, but he reminds me to always keep in mind that there will always be someone in better shape, faster, and more experienced. And conversely, there will always be someone slower and not in as good as shape. As I would learn, being just average on many levels would serve me well.

Part 3: And Then There Were 12

After a month of preparing physically and rounding up required gear, I am off to Aspen, where the events are more my speed: winter conditions, mountaineering, and skiing. As we did at Moab, we race. The first day, we race to the top of Highland Peak in heavy mountaineering boots. Again, I set a steady pace as I watch the field sprint out in front of me. By the top of the mountain I have passed many and again finish in eighth place. But, this time the field is smaller – only 24 athletes. We spend a sunny and warm day taking in the views of the Rocky Mountains, but more importantly, we are put through the paces to perform a variety of mountaineering tasks: zip lines, self-arresting, belaying, ascending ropes, rappelling. The works. This is easy for me, as I am experienced in all these things. I am amazed that many others have no experience in any of these disciplines but they are still in the running for getting to Everest, where these skills are a necessity. That night, we are split into teams and face two nights of winter camping and a 20-mile high-altitude, navigational ski traverse through the Elk Mountains. My team is a mixed bag of great experience and no experience.

The next morning dawns sunny, and we begin skiing up a mountain pass. Our team does well, but the inexperienced members sure try my patience with their wild and wrong ideas about navigating and finding our way through the mountains to the next camp. Just before nightfall, we cruise into camp and hunker down for a cold night. Our team had opted to save weight and only bring one tent, which we all now must fit into. This proves to be warm, but space is severely lacking. Several times during the night, I am awakened with questions on how to deal with the cold and altitude. Yet we all sleep well, for a few hours at least.

L-R: Troy, Sam Gehring, Petit Pinson, Jesse Haynes. Global Extreme friends in Aspen, Colorado. © Troy Henkels

Long before sunrise, and in frigid temperatures, we break camp and hit the trail. On the side of a desolate mountain, we watch the sunrise paint the Rockies every shade of orange and pink imaginable. As we continue to deal with the challenges of navigational issues, no one expects the several "surprise" scenarios that test our skills of first aid, avalanche, and emergency locator beacon searching. It is interesting to watch team dynamics unfold, not only in our team, but the others as well. And, of course, the experts are watching and taking notes the entire time.

After eight hours of skiing, we cross the finish line in third place. During TV interviews afterward, it is obvious that there is a lot of apprehension surrounding the selection of the final 12 athletes who would travel the world. That night, by bonfire, the experts announce who will continue on. My name is called! I have done it! I made the cut! For me, the news takes some time to sink in.

Sam interviewing with the camera crew in the mountains near Aspen.

© Troy Henkels

Part 4: Three Weeks of Frenzy

Back in Alaska, I have three weeks to prepare for the possibility of being gone for five months. Not only have I yet to ask for the time off work, there are bills to pay (five months in advance), gear to sort, physical conditioning, immunizations, and packing. Boxes of sponsors' gear show up regularly, and there are various media interviews. The "Global Extremes" director even sends a cameraman to follow me around one day and film my life at work and home. The entire reason this show is even happening is because of some big-name sponsors putting down big money. It is a bit overwhelming and unnerving in the beginning, but I eventually get used to interviews and having a camera around to record my every move. After a while, I don't even notice the cameras, and members of the film crew become my friends.

A bigger challenge is packing. "Global Extremes" will take us to Africa, Costa Rica, and Iceland – different types of environments – and we will be involved in a wide variety of activities, most of them ranging on extreme. After packing for some big expeditions, I had become meticulous and quite organized at packing. But this was on a far greater magnitude. The three weeks fly by.

It is during this time that I realize how big of an opportunity this is: High adventure all over the world, with someone else footing the bill. No matter what, it will be an experience to remember. Never do I have illusions of standing on the summit of Mount Everest; that is not the big draw for me. My attraction is traveling and experiencing new cultures and countries. Facing elimination at any stage, in any country, only time will tell what my fate will be. I am not really sure if "Global Extremes" was real or just reality TV.

Part 5: Endurance in the Kalahari

My bags packed, I lock the door on my life in Alaska. It is my 36th birthday, and I am flying to South Africa and the first stop on this around-the-world journey with "Global Extremes." Within the week, the first episode of "Global Extremes," filmed during the elimination rounds, appears on TV in the States.

Exhausted from 27 hours of travel, we land in Johannesburg and immediately board a small charter plane that will take us deep into the Kalahari Desert. Gazing out the window at the vast, sweltering landscape, I wonder if I could really handle the Kalahari. I have spent the better part of the previous decade in polar environments. I know nothing about the Kalahari, except that it is hot and dry. I also know that we would land in the middle of an African summer.

We land on a small, paved airstrip in the middle of nowhere. Stepping out of the plane, I am nearly knocked over by the heat. Even the 20 mile-per-hour wind blowing across the landscape is overwhelmingly hot. Our group is met by a band of Bushmen in native dress. We are amazed by how skinny and short the natives are. With cameras rolling, we spend an hour talking with these people and taking pictures. Someone has a Polaroid camera, which is a big hit among the Bushmen children, who are astounded to see pictures of themselves instantly.

We spend the first week learning about how the Bushmen live and survive in the desert. Not only do we learn about the people, but also about the environment and the creatures that exist in this forsaken land. The TV show's production company hired top-notch outfitters to cook and teach us how to train and perform in very hot desert conditions. We start slow and progress up to the levels at which we will need to perform. By Day 4 we are doing three-hour runs through the desert, stopping halfway to do wind sprints up sand dunes. I think I will die, as temperatures ranged from a "cool" 109 degrees Fahrenheit to a scorching 120.

All week, we learn from the Bushmen about hunting, tracking, and surviving. In addition, we learn from experts

Rappelling in the Kalahari.
© Troy Henkels

about nutrition, hydration, running, and driving a four-wheel drive vehicle to maximum performance. Throughout, we camp under clear, star-filled skies – and try to avoid scorpions on the desert floor.

In the second week, we are split up into teams of four for the duration of our time in Africa. It is time to race. Every day will have multi-sport endurance races, and our 2½ weeks will culminate with a 36-hour race. The losing team will have to eliminate one of their members.

My team is extremely strong. It consists of Sam, a multi-sport endurance athlete with some amazing races and triathlons under her belt, including Eco-Challenge; Eric, a Special Forces Marine and finisher of numerous Ironman triathlons; and Darren, an Outdoor Leadership instructor, Eco-Challenge racer and navigational guru. The interviews and filming are incessant and cannot be avoided. Often there is a cameraman with our team, usually working harder than us to haul heavy gear around and get footage as the team moves through various events using different modes of travel. We would be up before the sun and won't get to bed until late at night.

Bushman children checking out pictures from the Polaroid.

© Troy Henkels

There are short races and long races, always involving running, biking, kayaking, climbing, horseback and camel riding, and mostly navigating. Fortunately, Darren and Sam are both excellent navigators with experience in a variety of races and situations. My team, Shackleton (named after a legendary Antarctic explorer who happens to be a hero of mine) turns out to be the strongest in the field, but we don't race smart. We could move fast and far, but, due to internal conflicts, not efficiently. Nonetheless, we win every race except the one that is heavy on kayaking, where we are

eliminated because we lack all the required gear at the finish line. The other teams have their own problems, but the 12 of us will become great friends as we traipse around the countryside, racing and having fun.

In the process of all this racing, we explore the far reaches of the Kalahari, an immense place filled with wildlife, sand, and oppressive heat. Our races are always at a fast pace and amid high heat, usually around 120 degrees. Nonetheless, I am thrilled to have the opportunity. I start to enjoy the Kalahari and look at it as small snapshots of an amazing place. No matter how fast or far we travel, I know that I just have to keep up and endure the heat. For the most part I do keep up, without too much struggle – except for the race that started with a five-mile camel ride. That ends with me getting kicked in the leg by the camel. It hurt. It hurt a lot.

But what is more difficult is the subsequent 15-mile bike ride across blazing salt flats, followed by 12 miles of running and navigating in ankle-deep sand. By the end of the race, I wonder how much harder I can push myself through the heat and pain. Fortunately, the next day is spent paddling kayaks, and I am able to recuperate.

Our team is in first place going into the final race. It doesn't really matter because whichever team loses will be required to eliminate one member. The remaining 11 will go on to Costa Rica. With our speed, I didn't see any way that we can lose. The experts have warned us time and time again, that in adventure racing, it's not always the strongest team that wins. But we are undeterred. I am still concerned how I will hold up in the heat. We will have two solid days and one long night of high-endurance events. I had been on some long hikes and climbs, but nothing that compares to 36 straight hours of adventure racing.

L-R: Jesse Rickert, Colleen Ihnken, Eric Kapitulik, Tryntje Young, Petit Pinson, Darran Wells, Jesse Haynes, Sam Gehring, Andy Corra, Jan Fiala, Ted Mahon, Troy. Global Extremes team in the Kalahari Desert, Africa.

© Troy Henkels

Part 6: Final Exam in Kalahari

The race starts early in the morning with a long bike ride through vineyards, followed by several hours in kayaks down the Orange River rapids, and navigating on foot through a huge river gorge, complete with rock climbing and rappelling – all the time, working off maps and navigating with a compass to get to the next checkpoint. By mid-day, Team Shackleton is in the lead and going strong. There are countless hours along a river, on foot, in and out of the water to stay cool. Eventually there are several hours away from the river, while we sweat and hope for some relief from the heat. It finally comes. One part of the race requires us to sit in inner tubes on a river and paddle several miles downstream with our arms. It is bliss to be in the water during the heat of the day, even though, after several hours of paddling into the wind, I think my arms will fall off. After that, there is running in ankle deep sand. All the time, we are trying to stay nourished and hydrated.

At one point, Eric and Darren have run out of water – again – and we have to find a spot to fill up. It amazes me that these guys have consumed twice the amount of water that Sam and I have in the same amount of time. We fill up and think nothing more of it. By nightfall, we are on our bikes facing a 30-mile ride in the dark. I feel great and am ready to go, anticipating the cool night hours. Less than an hour into this bike ride, however, Darren starts to weaken and get sick. Before long, in pitch darkness in the middle of nowhere, he is on all fours, throwing up. Eric is not feeling well either. Later, we learned they drank too much water and the body's response is to flush itself. This afflicts Darren most of the night, and we watch our lead disappear. The other teams slowly pass us and gain a huge lead. For nearly six hours, Darren struggles along to the next checkpoint. There is nothing the rest of the team can do but be patient, compassionate, and let him recover. Our starry filled night is spent moving slower than a snail's pace, falling farther behind the other teams. By 4 in the morning, we reach the next checkpoint, where Darren has the choice to drop out or take an IV to rehydrate his system. He chooses the IV in hopes we can save the race by catching another team. Just before sunrise, we are on the trail again, climbing a 300-foot rock wall and then rappelling down. Back on our bikes, we labor through ankle-deep sand as the heat of the day builds. More running and navigating and pushing bikes in the scorching sun.

We move fast, but never fast enough for Darren, who wants to sprint to catch the other teams. He knows that if we lose this race, someone on our team will be eliminated – and he suspects it will be him. My feeling is that all we can do is keep a steady pace and hope for the best. Any more sprinting in this heat could overheat any of us and cause us to "crash" physically. We regain almost two hours on the other teams, but it is not enough. We are last.

In reality TV, drama is what every producer wants. So, at the finish line, exhausted physically and mentally, we are required to eliminate one of our teammates. There ended up being two days of drama revolving around this decision. For me, it is impossible to decide. All three of my teammates are extremely fit and talented. We have become friends. It seems ludicrous to assess their ability to climb Everest by some events we had done in the heat of the desert. Moreover,

Hanging out with Maggie, a domesticated cheetah.

© Troy Henkels

they are all elite athletes and very capable of taking anything on, individually or as a team. As a result, and much to the dismay of the drama-seeking director, I use a random game to determine I would vote to eliminate Darren. It is a tie vote between Sam and Darren. The experts ultimately decide to eliminate Darren – not because he got sick and lost the race for our team, but for his attitude after he had recovered and continued on.

In the course of all this, I am told they are having a hard time building a character out of me for TV. I take this as a huge compliment rather than an insult. Despite the pressures of being on TV, I am able to keep my personality and not let any of the production pandemonium affect me. Typically I'm a pretty quiet, middle-of-the-road, average Midwestern guy. Maybe my personality isn't fitting for TV drama, but maybe level-headed enough and very suitable for Everest? Time will tell.

With a sigh of relief I boarded a plane to leave Africa. The long days in the blazing sun were over and I had persevered. There would have been no disappointment had I been eliminated, for I had made some great friends and had an unbelievable experience. This alone was satisfaction enough for a journey. Yet, it wasn't over, as we flew under the cloak of darkness, headed east, across the ocean to Costa Rica.

Rappelling off a zip line in the Coter rain forest, Costa Rica.

Part 7: Costa Rican Bliss

The "Global Extremes" team has traveled halfway around the world, to Costa Rica. After an emotional and difficult decision in Africa, we are now a group of 11, from which a team of five will be selected to tackle Mount Everest.

Costa Rica is a different world from the dry, hot, sun-burned Kalahari Desert. Our first week is spent high in the mountains, in the rainforest, in the rain. Daily there is impenetrable fog and pouring rain. The resultant deep mud allows for spectacular scenes for the TV cameras.

In knee-deep mud we navigate through the dense jungle to find checkpoints in the middle of nowhere. During one event, two teams come across each other in the middle of the jungle and decide to travel together to find the camp where we would spend the night. Meanwhile, the other team is lost for hours, hacking its way through the thick underbrush with machetes. That night, as rain pelts our covered hammocks, we sleep to the sound of howler monkeys and a barrage of animal, insect, and bird sounds that create an eerie setting.

My team, down to three after dropping one member in Africa, is at some advantage because we are fewer and thus find it easier to make decisions, travel, and navigate. However, the downside is we have fewer hands and manpower when needed. By now, everyone is used to the interviews and cameras, but they are still everywhere. Costa Rica is so hot, humid, and wet that after the second day I will not have a dry stitch of clothing until we leave the country.

One of the more memorable events is a course set high in the rainforest canopy. Sixty feet off the ground, we travel through the canopy via zip lines. We clip into a pulley with a climbing harness and "zip" along cables from treetop to treetop. Each leg of the challenge requires new skills. At one point, there are two cables that we have to get our teams across – by walking on them. This turns out to be an amusing exercise in balance, trust, and teamwork. At other times, we have to rappel down the tree and climb back up another to get to our launching platform. Then off we zip again. On one line, I have to stop in the middle, drop a rope to the ground, rappel down, retrieve something, and climb back up the rope and carry on. Exhausting, but great fun.

We will race for two weeks and then have a long race as a finale in the last week. This time, each of the two losing teams of that race has to each eliminate a team member, no matter what. Team Shackleton is still very strong, but my two teammates do not get along. They are both very skilled in certain disciplines, like biking, running, kayaking, etc. But where one is strong, the other is weak, and vice versa. As a result, this prevents us from moving very fast. I constantly feel in a quandary of trying to evaluate my teammates on skills which have nothing to do with climbing Everest. It seems that athletic skills will not work for decision-making criterion. I will have to come up with something else, and this occupies my thoughts for much of our time in Costa Rica.

The second week is spent on a secluded beach on the Pacific. After the Kalahari, this is absolute bliss, complete with white sand, lapping waves, and spectacular sunsets. Even though all our gear is still wet from the humidity, it is nice to be in the sun and have the ocean to cool off in. All of our races involve water. We spend days running up and down the beach, kayaking, and swimming for long distances. It is hard to grasp the idea of traveling such great distances from our little beach and still return by nightfall. One race starts by retrieving map coordinates and instructions hung high in a coconut tree. Even with my extensive climbing experience, the hardest thing I've ever climbed was that damn coconut tree. We run long distances down the beach, and then swim across large stretches of water, only to find our kayaks and paddle lengthy stretches of open water to islands in the middle of the ocean, and then, on foot, circumnavigate the rocky shoreline. It is truly exhilarating and exhausting. Our last beach event, which will take us back to mainland Costa Rica, is a 22-mile open sea kayak race across Nicoya Bay. At sunrise, we start paddling. By noon we are still paddling, but now in eight-foot swells. Never in my life have my arms been more tired from the constant rotation of paddling. Shackleton finishes, and like hungry wolves, we devour fresh fruit at the finish line.

Part 8: Divide and Conquer

In the finale here, we will have a seven-day race called "La Ruta." It will take us from coast to coast, across the country. The race involves a variety of sports – many we didn't even know. We start on the Pacific side of Costa Rica, riding mountain bikes. With a festive send-off from the locals, the race begins with an uphill climb covering mile after mile. We head into the mountains on a course that is barely navigable from the maps provided. All day we ride, several times not knowing if we are still on course. At one point, two teams stop to ask directions from a small girl. In our broken Spanish, we learn that we are going the wrong way. Oddly, no one believes the child. We pedal five more miles, downhill, before we come across an adult; we believe him and end up riding back the way we had come – uphill and past the smiling girl who had given us the correct directions in the first place.

By mid-afternoon we are on foot, with a horse in tow, heading to the checkpoint where we will camp for the night. Our horse turns out to be injured and thus has one speed – unbelievably slow. It's just as well, as the mountain tracks are steep and the humidity is taking its toll.

In the morning, we split our team. Sam and I will canyoneer up a river drainage and Eric will take a mountain track and the horse, meeting up with us several hours later at another transition point. The canyoneering is nothing short of spectacular. Climbing up and down huge boulders, swimming the river, and climbing up waterfalls. Sam and I manage this without incident or injury, despite slippery rocks and strong currents. After rejoining Eric, we start the next stage on mountain bikes, on which we will spend the next two days riding a variety of terrains and races.

One section is a sprint race while another requires us to stop, shop, and carry all our food for the next leg of the journey. This leg finds us doing a jungle trek, testing our skills to work as a team and survive with limited supplies. In knee-deep mud and pouring rain, we camp along a small stream, using only a blue tarp as shelter and cooking the food we had bought the day before. It is a long, fun, and wet night, full of misery and mud.

Photo right: Climbing a coconut tree at the
start of one of the beach races.
© Troy Henkels

Hiking the next day through impenetrable jungle, we find ourselves atop a huge waterfall. We rappel down the face of the falls, jump from the rope into a pool of water and swim downstream until we can get out of the current and find a way through the boulders. We head back up the side of a muddy hillside and, for the benefit of the TV camera, look for poisonous snakes. Finally, by late afternoon we swim a large river and repack our gear in preparation for several days in kayaks. At nightfall, we camp along the famous Pacuare River. The entire next day is spent running rapids with the kayaks on the Pacuare and attempting to master a slalom course. This turns out to be great fun.

Three girls show up from across the river. They ask for me. I don't have a clue who they are. Maybe "Global Extreme" groupies? It turns out a friend from Alaska

Global Extremes team dinner in Costa Rica.   © Troy Henkels

is rafting the river and has noticed some Everest signs and wonders if this is the TV show I am on. Sure enough! It is such a pleasure to talk with someone who is unrelated to the show and to get some news from home.

The rest of our time in Costa Rica is spent kayaking on the Pacuare. We paddle rapids for several days through huge rock gorges, where waterfalls fall from high above. It is a truly a remarkable experience to paddle this river and experience it first hand, even if it is while racing. For the final day, we switch from river kayaks to sea kayaks, which are long, have a rudder and are built for speed. Our goal, and the race finish, is the Caribbean Sea, but little did any of us know how far away this still is. Long before sunrise, we start paddling. This time, there are few rapids, but a wide river with slow-moving water. We paddle all day, and slowly our team falls behind. Although we put in a good effort, the motivation just isn't there. Our fate is sealed. We will finish last and must decide which of us will go home. This decision weighs heavily on our minds as we cross the finish line. I know that my decision will settle the matter.

For weeks I have known that Sam and Eric couldn't be evaluated on skills or strength alone. Different criterion had to be used for my decision. I reflect on my climbing career and all the times I've had trouble in the mountains. I think long and hard about what factors created the problems. Always, it was communication — or lack thereof. Often, a break in communication is the downfall of a successful climbing expedition. When I evaluate Sam and Eric using this criterion, it is easy. Although Eric is by far stronger physically than Sam, his lack of communication with team members makes him a liability rather than an asset in the mountains.

We finish the race dead last. On a remote beach, in the wind, among piles of driftwood, near the pounding waves, the cameras roll as we announce who we vote to eliminate. Not surprisingly, Eric picks Sam and Sam picks Eric. As I suspected, my vote will determine it. I pick Eric. Eric never did say when he needed rest, food, or wanted to go slower even when there were countless times that I knew he desperately needed to stop and take a break. Sam and I always communicated our needs, wants, hungers, and shortcomings. That is an attribute that I feel is indispensable in high altitude mountaineering.

So it ends. Another team eliminates one member and we are now down to nine. Our next stop is Iceland for the final round, after which the team for Everest will be selected. Costa Rica has been difficult and fun, all wrapped up in one. Everyone is relieved that this leg is over.

This has been an experience to remember. I learn that sometimes in life, what seems like an obvious decision to some, isn't. Sometimes it takes looking at things in a little different light to make it all come clear. The trick is finding that light.

Part 9: Icelandic Dreams

People in their right mind would know better than to venture to Iceland in the dead of winter. But this "Global Extremes" competition was a dream trip, to places I had never visited, winter or not. I was thrilled with the prospect of finally being able to use my strongest skills. After spending 12 years in Alaska and enduring 16 months in Antarctica, cold-weather sports had become my forte. Certainly, I enjoyed warm environments, but since I was a boy, I have always been drawn to the snow, ice, and cold.

After arriving in Reykjavik, Iceland, our group flies north to the small town of Isafjordur, where new teams are selected and the focus of the event changes from racing to expeditions, which will be much more representative of what it would be like on Everest.

As was the case in the other countries, the first week in Iceland is spent learning about the local culture. This is perhaps the most fulfilling and fun week of my entire experience. My team of three lodges with a family, and we soon become close friends with them. Hjalmar, the father, is a power company lineman supervisor. Ran, the mother, is a teacher at the local elementary school. Herman, the son, is a sophomore in school and a star on the swim team. For a week we eat meals and go to work and school with this family, and learn what it is like to live in a remote village in Iceland. Due to Hjalmar's job, we see first-hand that Iceland exists largely on geothermal power. We are able to climb power poles high in the mountains during a severe blizzard, in white-out conditions. Several days are spent in school, talking to students about our travels and adventures and answering questions about George W. Bush and life in America.

Far before the light of day and in sub-zero temperatures, I walk with Herman to swim practice and swim laps, far behind the team. And, long after the light is gone, I venture to the school dance to learn that it is no different than when I was in school: Boys are flirting with girls and acting way too cool while Bon Jovi blares in the background. And, always, there is food – mostly food that is alien to me and sometimes scary. Ran takes great joy in concocting ways to make me eat things that I neither recognize nor enjoy. The worst is a traditional mid-winter dish of rotten shark. It is horrible, and I tell her so.

She laughs and makes the next victim give it a try.

My week in Isafjordur is a time that I will never forget. These friendly people live simply on the fringes of a very harsh environment. Unlike life in the United States, there seems to be little materialism and little unhappiness. Hjalmar, Ran, and Herman are simply happy with where they are in life and what they have. They take great joy and happiness in each other, and I am forever grateful they welcomed us into their home and lives.

Part 10: Stymied on Hvannadalshnukur

The competitors fly to the south part of the island and the glaciated mountain paradise of Skaftafell. In this part of the country, high jagged peaks loom over expansive glaciers, while waterfalls pour over cliffs and work their way toward the sea. The teams spend a long day on a giant glacier, practicing rope and climbing techniques that would be invaluable on Everest. These exercises are not only good practice for the athletes, but also an opportunity for the experts and guides to assess the skills of each competitor.

Feeling at home on vertical ice, I consider the most exciting part a ropes course traversing a section of the glacier. It involves ice climbing, rappelling, ascending the rope, passing knots, and crampon technique. It is old hat for me. In the ensuing days we prepare for an attempt to climb the highest peak in Iceland. Hvannadalshnukur is at 6,952 feet and a fairly technical climb involving hiking, skiing, and roped-up glacier travel. In order to get good footage, the production team wants us to spend the night high on the mountain. This poises the teams for a summit bid early the following morning, rather than climbing the peak in a day, like most climbers do. It takes an extremely long time to get film crew, production team, and athletes organized, packed, and started up the peak.

For most of the day we work our way up. By afternoon, we clip into skis and eventually crampons as we move onto glaciated and possibly crevassed terrain. The higher up the mountain we travel, the worse the weather becomes. By nightfall, we are setting up camp at 6,000 feet in frigid temperatures, a 40 mph wind, and a whiteout. The camera crew is happy to finally be getting some "extreme" footage.

Troy takes a break on Mount Hvannadalshnukur which,
at 6,952 feet, is the highest point in Iceland.
© *Jake Norton/MountainWorld Photography*

The weather rages all the next day, and we are pinned down in our tents. Every few hours, someone on my team has to brave the elements to shovel out our tent. Everyone does. By nightfall, the weather gets even worse, and our tent is buried beyond belief. Three of us shoveling at once cannot keep up with the snow drifting in. Our tent collapses under the weight of the snow, but I am able to retrieve sleeping bags just in time, so we can jump into other tents to spend the night.

The weather seems to be worse in the morning. At noon, the guides decide we should attempt a retreat. Visibility is minimal and we struggle to stay on our feet against the overpowering wind. It takes a long hour to dig out tents and pack up gear. With everyone roped up, we start downhill. We stop frequently – every time people are blown off their feet by the wind. This is a very long day, but our Icelandic guides, with the help of a compass, get us off the mountain and back to sea level. I am amazed that no one is hurt or lost, and even more impressed with the guides' abilities. We will observe their exceptional skills throughout our time in Iceland, as stormy weather and white-out conditions will be the norm.

After a few days of drying out and reorganizing, we are ready for the finale of "Global Extremes." It will be a six-day ski traverse across a large icecap, which will prove to be one of the most challenging events we'd go through. For me, this is a rare opportunity to travel across part of Iceland, on skis, in winter, with some of the finest people I've ever met.

We ski across landscapes covered with snow and studded with beautiful peaks. Since it is mid-winter, this playground is ours alone. There are no other people to be found. Many nights are spent in beautiful, remote huts situated near thermal hot springs. As the polar

Climbing ice near Skaftafell, Iceland.
© Troy Henkels

sunset colors surrounding peaks, and while we soak aching muscles in natural hot-water streams, the Icelandic guides regale us with stories about their land.

We have sunny, beautiful weather for two days – followed by a storm and some of the worst weather of our entire trip. Despite strong winds, cold temperatures, and low visibility, we are on a schedule and must keep moving. By this point, we are situated in the middle of the ice field and exposed to the storm. Each day starts out somewhat calm, but by afternoon we are struggling through the storm, fighting to keep hands and feet from freezing, as we search for our next hut or camping destination. The guides always find the way to our next stopping point.

Late on the final day, trashed and famished, we stumble into the last hut. The storm has only gotten worse as we descend off the ice cap. Visibility is only 10 feet. It is an impressive display of tenacity and skill by the guides to get us through this storm. Not only did they do it with professionalism, but also good humor.

During one afternoon, struggling to find our way to a hut, I am out front with our lead guide, Jon. I come up from behind to find him standing in confusion. His pants are around his ankles. It turns out that his sled had been rolling behind him, because of the wind and steep angle of slope. The cord pull on his sled tangled up, "grabbed" his Gore-Tex pants and yanked them down. He's unable to move and unsure what has happened. He smiles at me and says, "I think I need some help here." Jon is getting cold as blowing snow accumulates on his thin layer of long underwear. We unravel the sled and tangled line to release his pants. During all of this, Jon never falters nor shows any signs of stress. He calmly sees the humor in the situation, fixes it, and moves on. We finally reach the safety and warmth of the hut. Now we must vote off two of the nine contestants. I survive the cut. After that, the expert and guides will pick, from the remaining seven of us, the five adventurers who will make an attempt on Mount Everest. We all return to Reykjavik to warm up, dry out, and pack for home. The suspense lingers. Who will be picked?

The selection ceremony is held on our final night in Iceland, at an authentic oceanside Viking restaurant. The polar expert and our Everest guide announce their picks for the Mount Everest expedition. As my name is announced, the realization overwhelms me. Although I am beaming with excitement, the announcement is anticlimactic for me. I am tired and road-weary. We have been traveling all over the world, racing every day, for nearly three months. Even though this is an unbelievable experience, it has taken its toll – not just on me, but on everyone. The team needs some rest and down time. But the five of us headed to climb Everest have only two weeks to prepare. With excitement and trepidation, I head home to Alaska, wondering what the next two months will hold.

Part 11: Pondering the World's Highest Peak

At 29,035 feet, Mount Everest is the highest and, for climbers, deadliest peak in the world. Aware that I had climbed on North America and South America's highest peaks, people frequently asked me if I would attempt Everest. My standard response was, "Not unless someone else pays for it." Everest is also the most expensive mountain to climb. My opinion was that Everest had become a peak for extremely wealthy and often inexperienced climbers who were looking to cross the biggest mountain in the world off their list. This seemed to result in overcrowding and made Everest a very dangerous place. Nonetheless, a paid, guided expedition to Mount Everest is becoming a dream come true for me. I won't dream of passing up this opportunity.

Having just returned to Alaska after three months of racing all over the world, I am exhausted. This time back home whizzes by. Nearly every day, boxes show up on my doorstop. It is new climbing gear shipped by sponsors. Our lead guide has advised us to rest and put on as much weight as we can during our two-week break. But there is packing to do, taxes to file, and bills to pay. And, of course, if I hope to keep my job at the local phone company, I must think about showing up to work for those two weeks, before I leave again for two months.

Friends and family gush at me, "You must be so excited!" Who has time to be excited? Who has time to think about it? The reality of this reality TV show, and the upcoming expedition to Mount Everest, has not really sunk in. There is too much to do and not enough time to do it.

The view of Everest from base camp in Tibet.
Our climbing route is along the ridge on the left skyline.
© Troy Henkels

Part 12: Slow and Steady

Before I know it, I am airborne again, heading south and then west across the Pacific to Osaka, Bangkok, and, 26 hours later, Kathmandu, Nepal. My excitement for this trip is mostly about the places I will get to see, not so much for the climb. This trip will take me through Nepal and Tibet, places I never thought I would see. The bonus is the opportunity to climb on the famed, treacherous slopes of Mount Everest.

Our "Global Extremes" expedition will attempt Everest via the northeast ridge, the route that is more difficult and less popular than the southern route. As a result, it has less traffic. But because there is no icefall to traverse, it is much safer. The climbing is equally spectacular if not tougher, and every bit as dangerous in all other respects.

Our plan is to spend a week traveling into base camp (BC), so our bodies can acclimate to the extreme change in elevations. In high altitude mountaineering, if you do not spend ample time allowing your body to acclimate, it can kill you. From Katmandu, we fly into Lhasa, Tibet. From there we drive to Xigatse, Tingeri, and base camp on the Rongbuk Glacier.

The trip to base camp is an experience in itself. The towns, cultures, and landscapes are so different from my own. It allows me the rare opportunity to see and absorb another

The home of the Dalai Lama, the Potala, Lhasa, Tibet.   © Troy Henkels

way of life. Exploring the palace of the Dalai Lama, driving across the Tibetan Plateau, walking for miles outside of Xigatse, playing "kick the can" with a small boy in Tingeri, and getting my first glimpse of the Himalaya. Base camp on the Rongbuk Glacier is a vast field of glacial moraine, surrounded by 20,000-foot peaks, with Everest looming directly to the south. It is a beautiful but desolate location that will be home for months.

The five climbers on our team are exceptional athletes. Three of us have extensive climbing experience and have been on top of some of the world's highest mountains. The other two, although not climbers by nature, are in prime shape and have paid their dues in the mountains. In addition, there will be a guide, several Sherpa, and six cameramen. In total, almost 50 people will be in camp supporting our team of five climbers. In addition to cook staff, there are TV directors, satellite and microwave techs, commentators, and an array of production staff, not to mention one person in charge of the Toyota 4 Runners sent by a major sponsor. Unlike any other climb, which I organize on my own, this climb is different. All I had to do was show up. Camp is already set up, food is already prepared, snow is already melted for water, and our loads are already hauled. And, of course, we can never forget that this is not just a climbing expedition – it is a TV show.

"The Fab Five" L-R: Colleen Ihnken, Troy, Ted Mahon, Petit Pinson, Jesse Rickert.   © Troy Henkels

Part 13: Acclimating

After a few days of adjusting to life in base camp and 17,000 feet, our team starts climbing the surrounding peaks. Every other day, we climb a new peak, most of them around 20,000 feet. We climb high during the day and always return to base camp before night to sleep. This allows our bodies to adjust to the higher elevations that we will encounter on our ascent of Everest. Because this is all being filmed for a TV show, there are always interviews and filming responsibilities to take care of, so the producers can turn our climb into suitable fodder for television audiences back in the States. We spend alternate days from the hikes in base camp, organizing and repacking gear. Everything has to be ready for our assault on the mountain in the months to come. Soon, we will move to Advance Base Camp (ABC), while our gear must travel by yak, prior to our departure from base camp. With so much time on our hands, the team makes adjustments to camp. We will spend the better part of two months here, so it makes sense to make things comfortable. We collect lots of large, flat rocks to make a "porch" in front of each tent. This makes getting in and out of the tents easier and keeps out the dust. However, at 17,000 feet, the hauling is not so easy. Our heaving lungs search for oxygen that doesn't exist.

In base camp, I never tire of the phenomenal views of Everest at all times of day and night. Often, early-morning light illuminates fresh snow on the summit pyramid. In the afternoon, high winds blow the snow into a large plume, trailing off the summit. Late in the day, the wind subsides and the summit pyramid is bathed in a glowing orange, low-angle light. "Warm" is a relative term on Everest. Temperatures hover around freezing, and are often colder, particularly against the incessant wind. Of course, the higher up the mountain we go, the colder and windier it becomes. There is always wind. You can count on the wind. Most mornings, our team relaxes in the sun; there is little wind. By 10 a.m., we are scurrying for our tents or heavier down gear as the wind picks up, whooshing down from the glacier.

The boys on the way to ABC. Ted and Jesse would both end up summiting. © Troy Henkels

Despite all the activities in base camp, there is still a lot of downtime – plenty of time for reading, writing, games, eating, talking, and thinking. There are 14 other teams in camp, from all over the world and with several famous climbers, so it is fun to get to know some of the others on the mountain. Our team is on a somewhat accelerated program for acclimating, and everyone has good days and bad days. Typically, I return from an acclimating hike with a headache; that's not uncommon at these altitudes. One of the real challenges on Everest is staying healthy and maintaining an appetite. "The Fab Five," as the TV show production team likes to call us, are doing well in both respects.

After several weeks of acclimating climbs on smaller peaks, it is time to move to advance base camp (ABC). We will spend two days hiking the 12 miles and gaining 4,000 feet in elevation. The plan is to move up to ABC and do more acclimating hikes from there. We would start climbing the mountain, hoping to get as high as Camp 3 (25,912 feet), then retreat all the way to BC to rest before making a final summit attempt.

Advance Base Camp at 21,300 feet.   © Troy Henkels

Part 14: Knowing Your ABCs

The hike to ABC is up the moraine of the Rongbuk Glacier. We travel the same route as the yaks carrying our gear, and it is slow-going at this altitude and across rocky moraine. After two strenuous days, we reach ABC and it is like starting over again. We have to move into a tent, sort gear, and kill time while we let our bodies adjust to this new elevation: 21,300 feet. We spend several days lounging around camp, watching the wind blow plumes of snow off the summit. We listen in our tents at night as the wind, sounding like a jet engine, rages down on us from the North Col. The tent rattles so much that I am certain it will be launched with me inside.

Part 15: North Col and Camp 1

On our fourth day at ABC, we begin to climb. Using fixed ropes permanently attached to the mountain for safety, we ascend the steep slope to the North Col and Camp 1. From there, we will retreat to ABC and rest. A few days later, we will climb again, spend the night, and climb higher to spend

the night at Camp 2. High winds and low visibility hinder our trip up the crevassed North Col. To make matters worse, there are a lot of people on the route, causing traffic jams and dangerous situations. One problem with climbing on Everest is the sheer number of people the mountain attracts. Many people who can afford such an expensive climb have no experience in the mountains or at altitude. Large numbers of inexperienced climbers can create extremely dangerous situations. Another problem is that the fixed ropes can be extremely sketchy. New ropes are put up yearly, but the old ropes are not removed. So, facing a conglomeration of multiple ropes, a climber never really knows which are safe and which are not.

What has climbing on Everest become? Is mountain climbing really just pulling yourself up a rope that someone else put there? It boils down to several ethical climbing issues, none of which I had ever had to deal with on my self-driven expeditions in the Alaska Range.

Doing laundry at 21,300 feet is challenging   © Troy Henkels
to say the least.

Troy (on right) climbing up to Camp 2 on the North ridge of Mount Everest.   © Jake Norton/MountainWorld Photography

Despite all of this, by laboriously placing one foot in front of the other, we reach the top of the North Col and retreat to rest for a few days. Then it is time to climb back to Camp 1 at 22,960 feet. We have already been up this route, and there are no surprises. The climbing is spectacular, in sunny and relatively warm weather. Camp 1 is perched on the very top of the North Col. It has little flat space and mammoth vertical drop-offs on either side. As a result, many tents squeeze into its limited area.

After a restless night, we start toward Camp 2 at 24,600 feet. At first, this appears to be a short hike up easy terrain to the top of a long, narrow snowfield. There seems to be little technical challenge or difficulty. In Alaska, such a climb would take me an hour at the most. Not so in the Himalaya. It takes me nearly five hours. It turns out to be one of the most challenging things I have ever done.

As we climb, the air becomes thinner and the slope steepens. I struggle to breathe in the thin air and it is just as tough to put one foot in front of the other. I can manage only two or three steps before needing a break. It is exhausting, and it takes everything I have to reach Camp 2.

Camp 2 dug into the mountainside at 24,670 feet.

Part 16: No Margin for Error at Camp 2

Camp 2 is one of the wildest places I have ever camped. It is chipped out of ice on a very steep slope with just enough area for a few tents. There is no room for error here. Drop something and it is gone, sliding several thousand feet to the glacier below. If you fall, the same thing happens to you, and your chances of survival are slim. We spend most of our day at Camp 2 in our tents. We hide from the cold, rest, and prepare to go higher the next day. At this extreme altitude, everything takes longer. Even melting snow for our water requires an extreme effort. The altitude has killed my appetite and thirst, and I must force myself to eat and drink. Sleeping is difficult, and so I get very little. The upside of Camp 2 is the scenery. Our teams revels in the views of endless unnamed, unclimbed Himalayan peaks and a few notable ones, including Pumori and Cho Oyo.

In the morning, fighting high winds, we struggle to stay warm and reach Camp 3. We don't make it that far. The cold and wind force us to turn back and, as planned, we retreat to ABC to rest. I'm amazed, but the trip down is as difficult as the climb up. I can take only three steps before I must sit down and regain my composure. My body is thrashed. I'm exhausted. I need rest. After two days, we are back at base camp for at least a week of rest. Then we will watch for a weather window that will allow us to make a summit bid.

Photo left: The route to Camp 2 goes straight up the snowfield. Camp is just at the top of this snowfield. As viewed from the North Col.
© Troy Henkels

Part 17: A Big Decision

Meanwhile, I am struggling with a decision: Should I abandon the climb? After four days, I make up my mind: I am done.

I feel that, with more rest, I could go back up and likely reach the summit. However, I am not sure I could make it back down in good order. Not only could this be deadly for me, but it also could place my team in jeopardy. My body has been pushed as far as I feel is necessary. It has been a winter full of racing with very little recovery time, and I just don't have it in me to continue on safely. The scales on this decision tip for me when I considered what I would do in the same situation if I were on a small expedition in Alaska with a friend. I would go home and try again another year. This makes the decision easy.

I break the news to the team, guides, and TV production crew. They are quite supportive and understanding, and they note that the better part of climbing valor is knowing when to quit. I am relieved. For two more weeks, I stay in base camp with the team and help the TV production crew. My technical skills are of some use to them.

The team's summit attempt is thwarted at Camp 4 after they rescued another team's climbers who got caught in the dark on their return from a summit bid. Knowing the fatality rate is nearly 10 percent, witnessing near-fatalities, and encountering more questionable weather prompts two more members of the Fab Five to drop out. Even our guide abandons his climb after getting hit in the head by an oxygen bottle randomly launched from higher on the mountain.

Ted and Jesse, two of the Fab Five, from Colorado, endure for several more weeks, waiting out bad weather. In an amazing display of tenacity and perseverance, they finally reach the summit. By this time, however, I am back in Iowa. On a TV screen in Centralia, I watch it all happen, live, beamed via satellite. It brings tears to my eyes, seeing those guys standing on the summit and smiling.

In retrospect, I believe that it really wasn't important if I reached the summit. My experience was complete and one of a lifetime. I had been around the world, doing amazing things and forming some lifelong friendships. Everest will be there next year and the year after. It's not worth a life to reach the summit. I'd rather walk away, and, maybe someday, stand in base camp, again, and wonder what it would be like to stand on top of the highest mountain in the world.

Assessing ice conditions on the Bering Strait. The current here was moving at 5 mph!   © *Christian Hofmann*

CHAPTER SIXTEEN

SIXTY MILES ON THE BERING STRAIT

Part 1: Scouting expedition

Even before I wake up, my feet are dangerously cold and the wind hammers the walls of my tent. It is March – still winter 60 miles south of the Arctic Circle. The temperature hangs around minus-15 degrees Fahrenheit and the wind is blowing 35 miles per hour. Nonetheless, I consider it traveling weather.

I knew little about the Bering Strait when world renowned polar explorer Dixie Dansercoer asked me if I wanted to cross this semi-frozen strip of ocean on foot. I immediately said yes, as I often do when these opportunities present themselves.

Dixie and I met years earlier in Antarctica after he and a fellow Belgian had skied, unsupported and using kites, some 2,400 miles across that continent. We became friends over time, even though I had no designs on partnering with him on his crazy expeditions. When he came up with the idea to cross the Strait, I was the one he asked to join him.

The Bering Strait is a mysterious place. No one I knew had been there. It is so far out of the way, you really need a reason to go there. There are several expeditions a year to the Strait, during all seasons, but one hears very little about them because the success rate on the Strait is non-existent. Ice conditions and the weather are just too chaotic to offer much in the way of predicting what might go on.

A stiff wind on the Strait greets us on our first morning training near Wales.   © Troy Henkels

The rumors we heard are true. There is open water in the Strait. A lot of it. To deal with this, we have specially engineered sleds that not only take the abuse of being dragged through ice, but can float, fully loaded, and with us on top of them. Even better, when lashed together, they make a quite stable form of catamaran. We came up with the idea to rig a small sail on this craft in case we encountered long stretches of open water. Specially-made dry suits allow us to get wet, and even be submerged if necessary, yet keep us warm and dry.

To test it, I put on the dry suit and somewhat apprehensively climb into the Bering Sea with the current, icebergs, and 29 degree water. (Due to its salt content, the water does not freeze at that temperature). Surprisingly, not once am I cold or wet. If anything, I am too warm during the half-hour I spend swimming around and climbing on icebergs.

The weather is harsh, currents unpredictable, and the wind relentless. The Strait has only been crossed once on foot from Russia to Alaska. Dmitry Shparo and his son Matvey made it across in 1998 on their third attempt in as many years. After encountering severely broken ice, strong currents, and minus-30 degree temperatures, they were only able to average less than one mile an hour while traveling. They spent nine to 11 hours a day trying to make progress. Every day for the first week they encountered polar bears, and on several occasions they fell through thin ice and became totally soaked. Despite this, they persevered. After 21 days and traveling more than 186 miles, they set foot on land near Point Hope. They hadn't only made it across the Bering Strait, they essentially had crossed the Chukchi Sea.

In March 2004, Dixie and I fly to Wales, a remote north western Alaskan village and the United States' closest point to Russia. On a clear day, yes, you actually can see all the way to Russia. We are scouting conditions and testing equipment for an expedition the following year. Spending time in Wales allows us the opportunity to see what conditions are like in March. But mostly, we want to see the Strait. To do this, we must camp out. An inadequate sleeping bag provided by a European sponsor contributes to a cold and restless night. That morning, I need an hour and a half to get my feet warm before I begin to feel them again. Lesson learned: Don't let them get cold in the first place. In this environment, being that cold can turn dangerous quickly and without warning.

Part 2: How Hard Can This Be Really?

A year later, in March 2005, we are back in Wales. The task before us seems simple: Walk across the Bering Strait from Alaska to Russia and return by the same means. On a map, this small stretch of water separating continents and cultures is miniscule. But poised on the edge of continent,

Drysuit testing in the Bering Strait.   © Troy Henkels

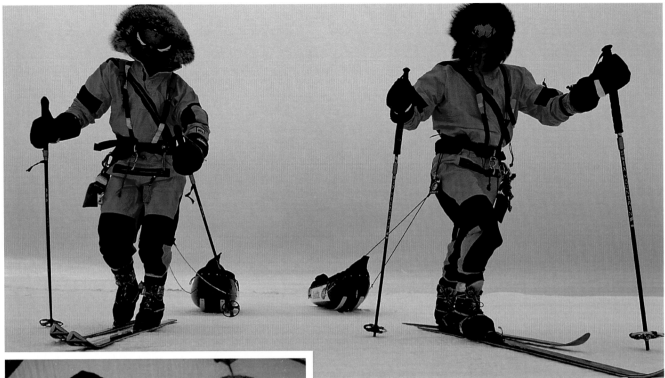

Traveling attire: Kōkatat drysuits, special boots, fur ruffs, and sleds that float.   © Christian Hofmann

Expedition team Troy and Dixie.   © Troy Henkels

looking west, we are confounded by the magnitude of such an endeavor. On the Bering Strait, it doesn't matter how many miles you travel as long as you travel all of them. How hard can it be, really? It's only 56 miles across from Alaska to Russia. If I had to, I can almost walk that distance in one day. Although we know about the hardships that Shparo endured on his crossing, we feel confident that we can be the first people to walk it from east to west, from Alaska to Russia. There has been no lack of attempts by others, but most expeditions attempting a crossing on foot last less than a day.

Like every good adventure, this one will entail a large element of the unknown. Dixie and I are not sure a crossing can be done, but we never believe it CANNOT be done, either. We both believe that with proper preparations, adequate training, and state-of-the-art equipment, we have a good chance of making it to Russia. And of course we need perfect weather, wind, and ice conditions. Without a doubt this shapes up to be the most dangerous and challenging journey of my career to this point.

After three years of difficult work – securing sponsors, modifying equipment, working out logistics, and whipping our bodies into shape, we are ready. Dixie and I are finally on the edge of North America, looking west into the unknown.

For 20 days, we restlessly wait in the tiny village of Wales and monitor the weather while storms pound in from the Bering Sea. A constant low-pressure system produces consistently bad weather and extremely windy conditions in the region. And it's wet. Due to the advent of global warming, the Strait does not freeze anymore, as it did a

We sail off at the start of the expedition, just moments before near catastrophe.

© Ellen J. Richard

century ago. The many currents that get compressed through the two land masses keep the ice in a constant, complex state of disarray. And it is cold. Very cold. Here, just south of the Arctic Circle, March and April is still a winter wonderland. So, in reality, we are battling three difficult elements – wind, water, and cold. Remove any one of those elements and this could be a straightforward expedition.

Part 3: Under Way and in Danger

Finally, noting a 10-day forecast for reasonable weather, and with 40 days worth of food, Dixie and I step off the North America continent and venture onto the Strait. Very few times in life can one begin something and not turn back. This is one of those times. Once we are on the Strait, we know we will have to make it across, be rescued … or drown.

We don't know which one it will be, yet we are ready and willing to take on the risk and adventure.

With a strong north wind to aid us, we ski to the edge of the landfast ice (ice solidly connected to shore). From here we are confronted with open water for as far as we can see into a fog bank. We lash our sleds together to form a stable catamaran and with a small sail and luck, we can cover many miles, with minimal effort.

This works perfectly for 45 minutes. Then ice floes around us begin moving with the current, compressing our area of open water. Within minutes, slush from all sides buries our sleds. Dixie and I recognize the danger of this situation, but there is nothing we can do. As our sleds become dangerously heavy with slush, much to our surprise, everything stops moving. We are stranded in a sea of slush, unable to move, with solid ice less than 30 feet away.

Preparing to cross a precarious section of broken ice.   *© Dixie Dansercoer*

Dixie attempts to ski across thin ice to safety, but the ice gives and he plunges into the water. Our custom dry suits save him from the frigid waters, but, without warning, the ice floes begin shifting again, threatening to crush Dixie or at the very least drown him in slush. Unable to remove his skis and swim, Dixie appears doomed. Fortunately, a quick toss of a rope and our quick movements get Dixie back to – and on top of the sleds. There is not a second to spare. Without speaking I remove his skis. Once again, the ice stops moving. We are still stranded. We edge our way to solid ice by kicking in the water and pulling through the slush with shovels. With great effort, we jump to a solid ice floe and eventually pull our heavy sleds to safety. Saying little, we disassemble the catamaran, hook into the sleds and start pulling, heading west, across stable ice and away from danger. I am shaken. Less than an hour into the expedition, we dodged catastrophe.

For several hours, pulling 200 pound sleds, we travel west as far as we can go. Confronted again with open water and slush, we see that we must find a different way. We travel for hours – north, south, and even east back toward our starting point. We are pulling hard through variable ice conditions and sometimes up and over 15-foot-high blocks of broken ice. We are surprised to cross ski tracks that we had put down earlier in the day. This is the final information we need. We are stranded on a very large ice floe, unable to travel in any direction due to open water and dangerous slushy conditions.

We set up camp for the night and talk about options for the following day. The GPS tells us that we have traveled only a few miles west and that the ice pack that we are on is moving 2 miles per hour … STRAIGHT SOUTH!!!! We quickly crunch the numbers. In the 10 hours that we will be camped, we will be pushed 20 MILES south! We will have to

Chaotic ice conditions make for difficult progression.
© Dixie Dansercoer

move quickly during daylight hours to counter this southerly drift and hope for a change in the wind and subsequent weather to allow us to gain mileage west toward Russia. There is no fooling Mother Nature.

On the second day, from the top of a large ice block, I can see no way to get off this ice floe. New ice had formed during the night near our camp, but it didn't look thick enough for travel. Dixie amazes me with his route-finding abilities and talent at reading ice conditions. Where I can only see roadblocks, Dixie finds a way. Through a maze of towering ice blocks and day-old ice, we manage to continue traveling west. Our progress is slow, usually only about one mile per hour. Despite both of us being in peak condition, in sub-zero temperatures, it does take a bit of effort to drag our 200 pounds of gear.

We never have consistent ice conditions. For an hour we will have large, jumbled blocks of blue ice that require us to push, pull, and finagle our sleds up and over. These pressure ridges then give way to flat, thick ice that is covered with two inches of slush yet to be frozen solid. The slush makes for a lot of friction under foot/ski and for heavy pulling. Open water often forces us to alter our course. Soon, we are back to a haphazard maze of ice blocks that can be navigated only with great effort.

We regularly take breaks to fuel our bodies with liquid and high-caloric foods and to check the GPS. It confirms that as we move west, we are also still drifting south – at a rate of one-half to 2½ miles per hour! – with the current and drift due to the persistent north wind. After about 10 minutes of rest, chill sets in and it is time to get back in motion to keep the internal furnace pumping.

Part 4: Off Course

The farther south we drift, the less stable and thick the ice becomes. Our map tells us that we are drifting toward King Island, a wind-swept and desolate mountainous island in the middle of the Bering Sea. As expected, one morning we look out from the tent and see King Island on the horizon. We hope to at least make landfall on the Island, for the sake of safety and possibly a potential pick-up location.

For several days, we try to reach this beautiful piece of rock, yet in the end we cannot, due to vast stretches of open water, slush, and dangerous ice. After two days, despite our exhausting efforts and despite King Island being just outside the front door of our tent, the current pushes us around and past it.

For seven days we have battled the Bering Strait, always moving west under our own power and also south due to nature's forces. In polar exploration, there is little room for error or wasted time, and our routines become systematic in everything we do: Set up camp, clean ice crystals out of clothing and boots, put on dry clothes, cook the food, melt snow for water, record our position and mileage, place the nightly phone call to our expedition manager (Dixie's wife, Julie), write the day's events for the website, etc., etc. In the morning, it is the same routine to get back in motion. These things have been second nature to both of us since long before we stepped onto the Bering Strait. We both have the skills and expertise to instill confidence and respect in one another.

By the seventh night, Dixie and I conclude that our expeditionary efforts are in vain. It's time to call for a helicopter pickup. Mother Nature is too powerful for us to overcome. With 60 miles behind us, we are almost straight south from our starting point, despite all the miles west we have labored. Now, with a storm in the forecast, we know it is in everyone's best interest to call for a pick up now, rather than wait and put ourselves in a rescue situation in the middle of a storm. Dixie calls Julie at our headquarters in Nome. We spend our last night on the Strait in quiet contemplation of how fortunate we are to have this experience in such a unique environment, a place very few people have the opportunity to experience.

By lunchtime on our eighth day on the ice, we are picked up by helicopter and flown to Nome. The flight takes us over vast stretches of open water and thin ice. This look from the air puts our small existence on the Bering Strait into perspective. Forty-five minutes later, with mixed emotions and no regrets, we land in Nome.

Part 5: Reflections

Though we didn't make it from Alaska to Russia, we did attempt something in the truest form of adventure into the unknown.

There are experiences during this expedition that will remain with me for a very long time: What it feels like to sleep with the sound of ice under pressure, screaming and groaning all night long in the distance. How your pulse races as you follow polar bear tracks through a maze of ice blocks. Wondering if you will fall through day-old rubbery ice as it flexes while you ski across it, in search of the elusive passage to the next maze. The realization that the ice floe on which Dixie is standing is moving away from mine – and reacting quickly so we get onto the same ice pack. Watching blocks of blue ice succumbing to the pressure of colliding currents and heaving 10 feet into the air. The feel of the north wind on your face first thing in the morning. Talking via satellite phone with your father, who is back in Iowa, while you are in the far reaches of the Bering Sea. Relying on your partner for your life. Watching the moon rise across a barren, polar landscape. Sleeping on moving ice, not knowing exactly where you will wake up. Realizing that failure is sometimes success in disguise. On no other expedition have I returned with such deep impressions of a place. The Bering Strait is funny and special that way.

Much later I realized it wasn't important how many miles we had traveled on the Bering Strait, but more so, how far I had traveled through life since I'd left Iowa more than twelve years earlier, in order to be able to set foot on the Bering Strait. With that, I sleep well at night, dreaming of all the miles yet to be traveled.

Our last moments on the Strait, just before the helicopter arrived.   © Troy Henkels

Postscript: The year after Dixie and I attempted the Strait, Karl Bushby and Dimitri Kieffer became the first to walk from Alaska to Russia, something that had never been done before. With very little experience, they completed the crossing in 15 days and were immediately arrested by Russian authorities for lack of proper permits. Like our attempt, their crossing did not come without its fair share of hardships and dangerous predicaments.

My brother Terry (right) and me practicing on my Dad's BMW for when we grow up.   © Pete Henkels

CHAPTER SEVENTEEN

TRAVELING THROUGH LIFE ON A BMW

Part 1: Faded memories

When I was born, my Dad owned a 1965 BMW R60 motorcycle. By the time I was 2 years old, I was a passenger on it. In the summer of 1969, my Dad took the family on rides to my Grandpa's timber, which was below Dubuque's old drive-in theater on U.S. Highway 20. When I say "the family," I mean that literally. At that time, there were five of us. Since I was smallest, I'd be the first on the bike, up front on the tank, holding onto the crossbar of the handlebars. Then came my Dad, driving and holding onto me. My middle brother, Todd, was behind Dad. Mom was next, holding onto Todd and Dad. Then came my oldest brother, Terry, seated behind my Mom and REALLY holding on. And whoever heard of helmets back then, anyway? In the saddle bags we'd pack a little grill and all the fixings for a picnic. We'd ride to my Grandpa's timber for the day to have lunch and play in the woods. I wish we had a picture of the five of us on that bike, but we don't.

My Mom died of cancer that winter, and Dad sold the bike a few years later. When I asked him why, he said he sold it because, well, he didn't ride it anymore. Apparently managing three boys on the bike alone was a bit much. Well, I hadn't considered that. My Dad was 36 then, just about the same age as I am now, by a few years. Now I own a BMW motorcycle (a 1998 R1100GS, to be exact). I never really planned to own one. I don't have many memories of my Dad's bike, so I don't know if it is just coincidence or inevitable that I got one.

Part 2: The allure and the lure

While visiting my friend Doug in the state of Washington several summers ago, he told me that he and a friend planned to ride their BMW motorcycles from Oregon to Tierra Del Fuego, on the southern tip of South America. The idea intrigued me. Doug was a bit put-off because their trip had to be postponed one year after his riding partner broke his back in a kite-surfing accident. During my visit, he let me take his BMW for a ride, and that only spurred me to ask more questions about his plans for an epic motorcycle journey.

Doug, knowing my passion for adventure and faraway places, lured me in, saying, "Well, if you get a bike, you could come along." I needed no further coaxing. Once back home in Alaska, I immediately began shopping online for motorcycles. There was one for sale near where my brother Todd lives in Arizona. He went to look it over and take a test drive, and, based on his feedback, I became the owner of a BMW motorcycle.

For the better part of a year, I outfitted the bike for a long overland journey. The biggest challenge was setting up the bike. With the motorcycle in my brother's garage in Arizona, and me in Alaska, this was no small task. It felt odd to be embarking on such a long trip on a bike that I'd ridden less than 200 miles, even though I've ridden motorcycles all my life. I'd have to rely on riding skills learned from my younger years.

A year later, Doug's original riding partner broke his back again – this time in a paragliding accident – and we nearly postponed the trip another year. It was finally decided that just Doug and I would proceed as planned. I was glad for that. I would have waited for another year, but I also know that life is short and opportunities such as this don't come around too often. A lot could change in a year, for Doug or me, that could further delay or even forever cancel a departure.

Doug and I just before leaving Phoenix, Arizona.

Part 3: Two for the Road

In early November, with bikes tuned and packed, Doug and I point our motorbikes south. We plan to be on the road for three months and ride all the way to Tierra del Fuego and back. We don't anticipate an easy trip, but it promises to be one rich in adventure, unforeseen circumstances, and foreign culture. Although there won't be five of us on this one BMW, thoughts of the old days on my Dad's motorbike would certainly ride with me.

Our idea is to get through Mexico as quickly as we can. Both of us have been to Mexico numerous times and we believe that we have seen everything there is to see. However, we fail to calculate the time and distance it will take to drive the length of Mexico, from the U.S. border to the Guatemalan border.

Our days are spent on the open road, exploring the West Coast villages while we work our way south along the Pacific. Each night before dark, we find an inexpensive but secure hotel or RV park to spend the night. Much to our surprise, we come across many "snowbirds," most of them elderly Americans and Canadians, who spend winters in the same RV parks year after year.

The most fun we have is in such a park just south of Mazatlan. It looks abandoned, but it turns out that everyone is poolside for Burger-and-Margarita Night. This is just what we need after a long day on the road. This park is filled with older people living like they are in their early 20s. They are so rambunctious about living and enjoying life, that it is contagious. We talk late into the night to some of the most fascinating people I have ever met. Yes, they are nearing the end of their lives, but you would never guess it. They are enjoying every minute they have remaining.

Farther south, we roll into Acapulco. It has been 20 years since I have been in Acapulco and I am amazed at how busy a place it has become. We can't find a reasonably priced place to stay, but we soon meet a guy named Dan, who invites us to stay with him. He lives near the center of town in a house that he inherited from his grandparents. It even has an indoor pool! Dan becomes our friend and tour guide as we linger in Acapulco, not really wanting to leave. But after four days, we know we have to get back on the road. During a downpour, we head toward Puerto Escondido, which turns out to be yet another paradise on Mexico's West Coast.

Part 4: A Change of Plans

By this point, we know that getting to the tip of South America is going to be a longshot. If we ride hard – really hard – for three months, we can pull it off. But it becomes apparent that taking our time and enjoying the countries and culture is more of what we are after, not traveling hard and fast just to make it all the way. We reset our goal to Panama and as far south as we can drive into the Darien Jungle.

We cross the border into Guatemala and some of the most lively and dangerous driving conditions I have ever experienced. No one in this country seems to know about road rules; if there are any laws about how and where to drive, they are largely ignored. The roads are in such a state of disrepair that it's hard to miss potholes. Add to that LA-style rush hour traffic everywhere you go, then you have a sense of what we are up against.

After 20 days on the road, we stop in Panajachel to see Doug's girlfriend, who is there taking Spanish lessons. This provides a much-needed break from the motorbikes, an opportunity to explore the area, and catch up on news from back home. This is a spectacular place, with 6,000-foot mountains rising around a beautiful lake and surrounded by terraced corn fields.

We hike one of the peaks nearby and are abruptly surprised when two military police carrying large guns show up. They are friendly enough – just on patrol of the trail – but it certainly reminds us that we are not in the U.S. any more.

Back on the road, we put down some long miles through El Salvador and Nicaragua. These countries are small enough that we can drive through them fairly quickly, and we don't linger much, figuring that we will spend more time exploring them on the return trip. With some apprehension we do explore a few back roads. We had read a plethora of scary stories about traveling in this part of the world, and if something is going to happen, it will be on one of these roads in the middle of nowhere. We make it through without incident.

Part 5: Bureaucracy at the Borders

By the time we reach Costa Rica, we are fed up with border crossings. Throughout Central America, they are a challenging and time-consuming affair. Each crossing is pandemonium, with loads of people wanting to help you through the process – for a small price, of course. Our problem is that it's not readily obvious what the process is, and where certain offices are. It usually takes us two or three hours at every crossing. Not only do we have to see Immigration to have our passports stamped, but we also have to see a few other officials to get vehicle permits for the motorbikes. It usually takes visits to up to a half-dozen offices to get everything done.

First we have to see Immigration to exit a country. Then another person to check our vehicles out of the country. Then we have to see Immigration of the country we are entering. Then the vehicle people. These offices are never located in the same building – or even near each other. There is always a line at each place. Sometimes there is a fee, often payable only in local currency, which means that we must find a bank and wait in line again. And you always need photocopies of everything; even if you have enough copies, you always need more. Sometimes the motorcycle tires have to be washed and disinfected.

And, of course, everything is manual. There are very few computers involved. Doug and I develop a good routine: One of us deals with all the paperwork and offices while the other watches the motorcycles and fields questions from curious onlookers.

The most interesting government office is one Doug has to find. It is in a small non-descript building with no signage, and he must squeeze around a telephone pole just to get in the door.

Costa Rica is so Americanized that it is easy traveling and user-friendly. The beaches are great for surfing and the towns along the coast offer a lively night life. Although the roadways are fairly busy, the motorcycle riding is relatively safe. Nonetheless, the police or military stop us every day – not because we are doing something wrong, but because we look like wealthy Americans on big fancy bikes. One officer stops us for speeding in a hospital zone. He waves us down from the side of the road, standing next to his motorcycle, which is in dire need of repair. It has a small hand-held speed detector haphazardly wired into a cigarette lighter. There are no speed limit signs around, but in broken English and Spanish, he threatens to haul us off to jail if we don't pay an $80 fine, which is really pocket money for him. We refuse and that starts an hour-long standoff. We win. He loses patience and realizes he won't be profiting from us. He lets us go, but not before a lively and fun conversation in which he laughs in my face and tells me I look like a wimpy George Michael. Slightly offended, I ask him if he knows "Ponch" from the popular American TV show "Chips." He looks just like Ponch. But this falls flat because he's never seen the show. Finally, like our best friend, he wishes us well and sends us on our way.

Taking a break in Panama City, Panama.   © Doug Stroop

Part 6: Panama and the End of the Road

I set a new world record getting through the border from Costa Rica to Panama: an hour and a half. It is Sunday morning, and not so crowded, so things go pretty smoothly. Panama seems to be really well organized compared to all of the other countries. Doug and I are surprised and impressed with Panama's landscape and roadways. We are confronted with a four-lane highway all the way to Panama City through lush jungle and mountains. After all the other dilapidated roads we'd traveled, we find the bikes really like going fast on these sorts of roads. We find a nice beach about an hour outside of the city. It is called Santa Clara, and it turns out to be a beach as far as you can see in both directions. It's the best beach we have come across. It costs us $2 to pitch our tent under a thatch roof, right on the beach. Sodas are 65 cents and beers cost 80 cents. We have landed in paradise just by happenstance. I would be willing to stay right here the rest of the winter.

Crossing the Panama Canal is a milestone for us. It is something we focused upon the entire trip. It is hard to imagine that we have actually made it this far. Panama City reminds us of Miami, with lots of people, traffic, and skyscrapers everywhere. South of Panama City, we drive as far as we can into the Darien Jungle district. We have received many warnings about it being unsafe in the jungle, including impassable roads due to recent rains. We find that none of that is the case. It is very scenic with very little traffic. We are able to see some of the most indigenous and primitive people that I have encountered anywhere in the world. It is astounding to see primitive shacks built on stilts and people living, not in poverty, but very modestly.

The farther south we drive into the jungle, the more intense the guns and military presence becomes due to the serious drug trafficking from Colombia. No one at the last checkpoint is happy to see us, and they look at us suspiciously. We drive until we can drive no farther. The last 10 miles involve roads so muddy that we can't continue. After that, there is no road, just foot trails all the way to Colombia. We have made it as far as we can in the Darien Jungle. Now, all there is for us to do is point the motorbikes north and head home.

Part 7: Homeward Bound

The return trip north is equally exciting. In Costa Rica, we navigate some of the wildest, scariest bridges I have ever been on. Several old train bridges with random boards placed between the tracks are used as a regular roadway. The problem is that many boards are rotten or missing, and on a motorcycle, one mistake can mean disaster. Driving across these bridges is unbelievably nerve-wracking. My pulse races when I see Doug wipe out and lay his bike down. Fortunately, he lands in the middle of the tracks and is unharmed.

Honduras turns out to be a surprise and a treat. Beautiful mountains, twisty roads, friendly people, and so many shades of green that it's hard to describe. We spend an unforgettable night on the shores of Lake Yojoa and then explore the Mayan ruins at Copan. Back in Guatemala, we drive over a mountain pass through pine forests and just about freeze as we top out at just under 10,000 feet. It is on this road that we narrowly avoid several head-on collisions.

Ride complete, back in Tucson, Arizona.   © Troy Henkels

The first involves a bus passing a line of vehicles while going uphill around a blind corner just as we are coming around the corner. The driver doesn't slow down or even seem to notice us. In the lead, I am barely able to maneuver the bike onto the narrow shoulder. Fortunately, Doug is paying attention, and he also gets out of the way without hitting me. Without this narrow shoulder on this road, we would have been doomed. We were lucky: Most roads in Guatemala don't even have a shoulder.

We are happy to get out of Guatemala alive and back on the seemingly sane roadways of Mexico. But in Tehauntepec, traffic is backed up at a river bridge connecting two towns. Hundreds of people walk back and forth across the bridge. It turns out that there is some sort of political uprising, and they have the bridge closed on the other side and will not let any traffic go in either direction. Some folks say it will take hours or even days for the problem to be resolved. Feeling that the situation could turn tumultuous quickly, we move on. We find a dirt path down to the river, riding across the gravel river bar and crossing the river in several sections. We are back on the road on the other side and on our way. We skip Acapulco and take a different route through Mexico, visiting some quaint old colonial towns and silver mining districts. As we had on the trip down, Doug and I underestimate Mexico. We really enjoy it.

Finally, after months on the road, we cross the border back into the United States. It is raining and snowing as we enter Arizona. I have never been so cold as I am riding those several hundred miles to a friend's place in Tucson. The next day, I bid farewell to Doug and drive to my brother Todd's in Phoenix. When I pull into his driveway, it is like I'd never left. He says, "Well, there you have it," smiles, and welcomes me home after 10,000 miles on the road. It has never felt better to be on familiar ground. My BMW motorbike, like my Father's, has provided me with memories that will last a lifetime.

Postscript: Several days after returning to Arizona, on my 39th birthday, I ended up in the emergency room. Unbeknownst to me, at some point on the trip, a small organism embedded itself in my intestine and was wreaking havoc on my digestive system. The doctors didn't notice it at first, but days later they figured it out and put me on the right drugs to rid it from my system. If it had gone unchecked, the organism could have killed me. I lost 15 pounds, and it was three months before I was back to normal again.

Cranking out the miles on the Fireweed.
© Jan Houser

CHAPTER EIGHTEEN

FIREWEED

It wasn't so long ago, it seems, when my close friend Jody, who works in the bicycle industry, said something about "Lance." He was appalled that I had never heard of the guy. He enthusiastically told me all about Lance Armstrong, and I started watching the Tour de France. I have ridden bicycles all my life. As a kid I explored every gravel road within 20 miles of my Dad's Iowa apple orchard. All of this on an old 10-speed that Dad bought for me at a garage sale. That 10-speed stayed with me until I graduated to a Fisher mountain bike upon moving to Alaska in 1991. Finally, in 2006, I got the bug and decided to buy a road bike. I really like being out on the open road, being exposed to the elements and exploring open landscapes.

My interest in road biking isn't so much to race but to just ride. However, I became aware of a race that seemed like a pretty good challenge: The Fireweed, a 400-mile race across some of the most beautiful landscapes in Alaska, from Eureka to Valdez and back. Four hundred miles sounded like a lot for my first race, and my better judgment told me I should enter the 200-mile division of the same race in the first year and maybe step up to the 400-miler in the second year. I bought a discontinued Klein Q Pro, all the riding gear, and signed up for the 200-miler. Without knowing much about pelotons, and having never been on a group ride, I figured it was better to enter the non-drafting division and play it safe. With my lack of road-biking experience, there was no way I could hang with a group of serious riders.

Springtime in Alaska is like winter in the lower 48 states, so I didn't get in many training rides. Sometimes it's June before we have dry roads. By then, I was training to run my first marathon, so I didn't have time for long training rides. I finished the marathon two weeks before Fireweed, so I started riding. I got in some good forty and fifty mile training rides, which seemed like enough to me. A few friends who are serious riders sort of cringed at my training regimen – or lack thereof. While they were keeping track of cadence, watts, heart rate, speed, and torque, I was just out riding on the open road, having the time of my life.

The morning of the race, my friend Jan, who had volunteered to be my "road crew," and I drove 1½ hours into the mountains to the starting area. I didn't want to be late, and we arrived shortly after 5 a.m. even though the actual race didn't start until 8. I stood around, shivering, for about 10 minutes when a race official told me that if I was in the non-drafting division, I could start with any of the other divisions; they were starting every half-hour leading up to the main drafters' departure at 8 a.m. That certainly made sense to me. I preferred to ride alone anyway, and my race was really only against the clock, so why not start early? The sooner I started the sooner it would be over. So I mounted my bike and left with the next group.

Jan and I worked out a system that she would drive ahead about 20 miles and wait for me. She would watch me pass, see if I needed anything, and then go another 20 miles or so. This allowed me the freedom of the open road, and she got the solitude she sought in a weekend away from the city. This plan worked perfectly, including the one flat tire I had. I flatted out soon after passing her. She pulled up just as I finished putting the new tube in, pulled out the floor pump, and I was back on the road in no time. Throughout, the sandwiches she handed me as I flew past were just what I needed to fuel my body for the entire 200 miles.

One thing about Alaska weather: It is usually miserable. It was chilly when I started shortly after 5 a.m., but the sun came out for about 40 minutes, lighting up the landscape in a spectacular display. Then it started to rain. And continued to rain. Not just a sprinkle, mind you, but at times a heavy downpour. With my head down, I turned up my iPod and kept pedaling. Hours and miles went by in a blur. One thing was for certain: I was having a good ride – or better put, a fun ride. Winning or even competing didn't matter, I was just glad to be pedaling through some pristine mountain countryside, albeit in a downpour. I was cold, but I hardly ever noticed. My riding shoes had not seen enough miles to really be broken in, so I was glad my feet were numb to the point of feeling like blocks of wood. If I had been able to feel my feet, I would have been in agony from the new shoes.

The route took us on a long, slow climb up Thompson Pass just north of Valdez. In the rain, I reached the top and started the 20-mile descent into Valdez. No bikers, from any division, had caught me yet, and I slowly started passing several 400-mile riders who had started several hours before me. I was impressed that, by the end of the race, they would double my mileage.

Cresting Thompson Pass in bad weather.   © Jan Houser

After 200 miles and 10 hours and 27 minutes, I crossed the finish line with a smile on my face. My first real road race had not only been fun, but was relatively painless. And it was over. I went straight to my hotel and jumped in the hot tub. After an hour, I felt warm again. I headed back to the finish line to watch the other divisions finish. The most fun was watching the drafters sprint to the finish. They completed the course a little under an hour faster than me. Later that night, when the race organizers posted all the times, I was astonished to learn I had won the non-drafting division! The second-place finisher was only eight minutes slower. Although I'm not super-competitive, it is always a good day when you can ride some long miles, feel the freedom of the open road, and at the end of the day wind up in first place. It doesn't always work out like that for me, of course, but on that rain-filled day it did.

Fireweed and Trail Lake, Alaska.   © Troy Henkels

Detail of the upper half of Pioneer Peak.

CHAPTER NINETEEN

RUNNING WITH SCISSORS ON PIONEER PEAK

© Troy Henkels

Springtime in Alaska can be glorious. The sun starts to feel warm again and the days become noticeably longer. One spring, I planned another attempt on a mountain that had been defying me for several years. At 5,398 feet, Pioneer Peak is not particularly high, yet it towers over the farmland that sits just above sea level in Palmer Valley. This peak offers such a drastic and dramatic north face, it was hard for me to imagine anyone climbing it. I knew it had been climbed, but I could not actually find anyone who had climbed the north side.

I started my assaults on the north face of Pioneer Peak several years earlier. In several attempts over a two-year period, I had only made it a little above halfway. Common sense always turned me back due to dangerously steep rock walls, newly formed ice and wet and slippery terrain. My failed attempts were adding up. Unclimbed mountains tend to haunt me, and Pioneer Peak was starting to gnaw at my psyche. So I found myself gearing up for another attempt. This time, I opted for safe climbing and packed crampons, short and long ice axes, climbing harness, rope, and numerous anchoring devices. However, due to my not-so-good common sense and desire to travel fast and light, I left all this equipment in the truck, except one ice axe and crampons. My reasoning was that if I encountered any dangerous terrain that required more gear, I would retreat and chalk it up as another failed attempt.

Because I am traveling with little gear, I make quick time up the lower ramparts of the mountain. Although strenuous, it doesn't pose any real threats or extreme technical difficulties. About halfway up, I reach a long, steep snowfield. The sun is slowly working its way around the mountain, warming things up and making the snow surface heavy and somewhat avalanche-prone. Despite this, I think it is still safe enough, and so I keep to my pace. As I climb higher,

Pioneer Peak on a summer day with the climbing route indicated.

© Troy Henkels

I end up in a natural chute that will take me straight up the daunting crux of the north face.

It is here, to my surprise, that I came across other climbers' tracks. I can't believe it! What is the likelihood that on any given day, on a random peak in Alaska, someone has gone up before me? This doesn't thrill me, but as I scan the rest of the route, I can't see anyone, and haven't heard anything, so chances are good they are already on top and maybe descending via another route. Nonetheless, I am grateful for the boot trail they have put in, as it makes the going relatively easy compared to breaking trail in heavy snow, as I have been doing. I churn out the next 1,000 feet relatively quickly. There are several sections of rock and ice that are at the upper level of my climbing ability. Midway through one of these, while looking below, I realize I will not be able to retreat down what I was climbing up without

a rope – a rope that is still in the truck. So I will just have to find another route down.

It dawns on me that whoever it is ahead of me are pretty good climbers. They are getting up some rather technical and dangerous vertical rock and ice. I figure if they can climb it, so can I. What I don't know at this time is they are climbing with ropes and anchors, thus protecting them from a fall.

The beauty of mountaineering is it offers a wealth of time for self-reflection. I thought of words from my close friend Maggie, who once told me, "You don't play well with others and you like to run with scissors." I had an idea of what she was trying to tell me, but I didn't really understand or give it much thought. Now I understand. She is right: I don't play well with others. She certainly wasn't implying that I don't get along well with other people, but more simply that when I go into the mountains, I usually do it alone. That is

144

true. That is how I prefer it. I started at a very young age, alone in the Iowa woods, honing my outdoor skills. Despite the inherent dangers, I feel safer traveling alone; there is less stress when there is only me to worry about and I can travel more quickly.

"You like to run with scissors." Certainly, Maggie has a point here as well. There are times when I take risks in the mountains … akin to a child running with scissors. At no other time is this more apparent than now, while clinging to the north face of Pioneer Peak. But I'll have to worry about fixing those things later. Now, I must concentrate on getting up and down this mountain in one piece.

After climbing up several precarious and un-retreatable pitches, I come across the two climbers who have so graciously been breaking trail for me the last thousand feet. Mike and Dani are spent. They are hauling a lot of gear, which keeps them safe but also makes this climb a real battle. It has slowed them to a snail's pace. They are ready to retreat. They are so worn out, they think it is better to give up and retreat than try to struggle up the last thousand feet of near vertical ice, snow, and rock. And the heat of the day is making our entire slope a big question mark in terms of avalanche danger.

The least I can do is break trail for them for the last thousand feet, as they had done for me the previous thousand. I know the difficulties involved with getting up this face, and retreating this close to the top seems pointless. They agree to press on. I take off in the lead.

This final push to the summit of Pioneer Peak genuinely scares me. Climbing up extremely steep, avalanche-prone gulleys is sketchy at best. The summit ridge is windblown, and it demands full-on concentration. One wrong move could mean a fall off either side of a very narrow ridge. I make it to the top.

However, on the climb up I realize that it is going to be too dangerous for me to descend solo the way I had climbed up. It makes sense to try to descend down the back and, supposedly, easier side of the mountain. But the weather has slowly deteriorated. As I stand on the summit, looking for a possible escape route, I know it will be a very risky descent in windy, cold, and whiteout conditions, especially on a ridge that I had never been on. I was in dire straits.

About this time, Mike and Dani reach the top. They are ecstatic over reaching the summit. They thank me for convincing them to keep going for the summit and they offer to let me use their rope and anchors to descend. The success of their climb depended on me, and oddly, the success of my climb is still dependent on them if I am to get down safely. In unspoken words we realize how lucky we are to have each other on top of this Alaskan mountain. Despite the adverse weather, we manage to get down without incident. Without a doubt, this has turned out to be an epic climb. I am glad it is over.

There was a good lesson for me in this climb. Sometimes in life, if you are going to run with scissors, it might be a good idea to play well with others. Because often, all you really need is a little help from your friends.

Winter flying in the Chugach Range, Alaska.
© Troy Henkels

CHAPTER TWENTY

I LOVE THE WIND

Soaring over Turnagain Arm on the outskirts of Anchorage, Alaska.

While packing up my gear after an afternoon of kitesurfing on Resurrection Bay in Alaska, I reflected on what makes me pursue such unique activities in so many unlikely places. Kitesurfing, which is much like windsurfing but utilizes a kite to generate not only power but also lift, was my latest passion. For a year, I had a vision of how spectacular it would be to kitesurf on this bay surrounded by pristine mountains, glaciers, and ice fields. There were some obstacles, like where to get the gear and how to kitesurf. And there was the ever-present question surrounding many of my passions: Can it be done? Nothing like this had been done here, with its wind, rocky beaches, and very frigid waters.

All these things make water sports not very popular in Resurrection Bay.

Playing in the wind is something I have been doing all my life. My fascination with the wind started at an early age and has stayed with me all over the world. When I was 8 years old, my excitement peaked when my industrious Father suggested that we build a kite. After a trip to the library for a book on kites, I was ecstatic when I picked out a picture of a simple box kite, and my Dad said we could build it. We started building immediately and, to my amazement, it flew marvelously. However, it got better. My Dad always

148

had creative and bigger plans for most projects, and this one would be no different. With the help of two older brothers, we built a six-foot, pyramid-shaped kite of thin wood and paper. From a child's perspective, it seemed impossible that such a huge kite could fly. Construction came off without a hitch. The question was: What sort of line would hold such a massive kite when it is airborne? With all his engineering savvy, Dad came up with a spool of thick line that we somehow determined would be light enough to fly, yet strong enough to hold the kite.

On a chilly late-fall afternoon, with a classic Iowa storm heading our way, we went to the park to test our kite. It flew! It climbed higher as we let out more line. Before long, the wind gained strength and broke the line. We watched the kite spiral out of control and smash into a million pieces when it crashed to the ground. No one was disappointed, though, as we had our fun in the engineering, contemplating and constructing the kite. What the wind had done with this giant kite only fired my imagination. My fascination with the wind was firmly set by this point.

My fascination with the wind grew during my Iowa summers windsurfing with best friends Dale and Jody at Boy Scout Camp in Colesburg. Windsurfing was new then, so we had to learn by doing, and we spent endless hours on the lake figuring it out. Before long, we were zipping around, having fun, and always looking for that perfect wind day. As the summer wore on, our days were often dictated by what the wind might do.

When I was in college, my friend Lupo found a plywood boomerang at the local sports shop. We became determined to master these strange pieces of wood. And we did. Not only could we get them to fly, but we figured out how to make them come back – and even catch them when we were brave enough to try. I spent one Christmas vacation constructing multiple prototypes of boomerangs. Even today, I still have about 10 boomerangs, and I always travel with one. I have thrown them all over the world.

When I began exploring Alaska mountaintops and watched eagles, hawks, and falcons soar, I dreamed of doing the same. Paragliding was the answer. Much like hangliding,

Kitesurfing on Turnagain Arm.   © Troy Henkels

Late night kitesurfing on Turnagain Arm.

© Steve Conger

paragliding uses a parachute-like wing that packs into a small backpack one can hike with. This means of portable flight had me hiking up every peak just so I could jump off and fly down. This passion went around the world with me, allowing me to fly like a bird in Alaska, Iowa, Arizona, Oregon, Washington, New Zealand, and Australia. I have found nothing that compares to soaring with eagles and the bird's eye perspective offered from just below the clouds.

In Antarctica, I watched a hearty explorer leave the South Pole on skis, being pulled along by a kite. I was hooked. Borg Ousland became the first person to do a solo, unsupported traverse across the continent. It took 99 days.

Before long, I was cruising across the Antarctic landscape at speeds approaching 45 miles per hour. Once again, I found the wind fueling my passion.

Most recently, my fascination with the wind has involved kites, surfboards, and the cold waters of Alaska. My interest with kites from the years of my youth has come full circle, as I kitesurf anywhere I can and at every opportunity. It has shown me that, the things we learn early in life often end up shaping the way we live our lives. Somehow, the small things in life have the potential to manifest into great things – sometimes when you least expect it. Flying kites has allowed me to pursue my fascination with the wind, well into middle age.

The Belgica sailing near the Lemaire Channel.

© Laurent Dick/www.sailantarctica.com

CHAPTER TWENTY-ONE

IN THE WAKE OF THE BELGICA

Dixie called from Belgium and asked if I would be interested in being the cameraman on a sailing expedition to the Antarctic Peninsula. The expedition was going to commemorate the first Belgian and purely scientific expedition to Antarctica, which sailed 110 years ago. It would be a small crew, on a small boat, and probably be quite challenging. Like all decisions in my life that hinge on once-in-a-lifetime opportunities, quickly and without much contemplation, I said yes.

Dixie had secured sponsorship money and recruited a multinational crew. He also had lined up a steel-hulled 47-foot sailing yacht, renamed the Belgica to commemorate Adrian de Gerlache's expedition in 1890. Not only would we sail the southern seas to commemorate the original Belgica

expedition, we would also make the same 20 landings that Gerlache had made. However, when our 20 landings were done, we would have time for our own explorations and fun. Our destination, the Antarctic Peninsula, is a playground for adventurers who love the mountains and the ocean. Dixie and P.J., our communications man, were windsurfing buddies from their younger years, so windsurfing gear was a necessity on this trip. But I also wanted to bring kites.

My windsurfing days ended in 1996, when I discovered snow-kiting. I was working at Amundsen/Scott South Pole station, and I saw Norwegian Borge Ousland depart to make the first solo crossing of the Antarctic continent. I watched him put a kite in the air and away he went, using the wind to pull him along. At the time, I never imagined I would return

Blue iceberg waiting to be climbed.
© Laurent Dick/www.sailantarctica.com

A view from the mast. © Laurent Dick/www.sailantarctica.com

L-R: (back) Troy, Laurent Dick, Michel Tordoir;
(middle) Dixie Danseroer, Pietierjan Kempynck;
(front) Rumen Grozev. The Belgica team.

© Laurent Dick/www.sailantarctica.com

to Antarctica more than 10 years later, not to snowkite, but to attempt to kitesurf on water.

I keep meticulous journals. Sometimes, my journal entries tell a better story than me trying to retell it later. Here are a selection of journal entries from the In the Wake of the Belgica Expedition.

24 December 2007 – Ushuaia, Argentina

There is excitement in the air. Not too many times in life can I say I've been standing on the edge of an expedition to Antarctica. Our goal is to revisit each of de Gerlache's 20 landings and compare the ice mass at each location as well as to document atmospheric and wildlife data. This has inspired a similar viewpoint for everyone on board the Euronav Belgica, one of a charmed existence at our good fortune to be here. But first, we must cross the Drake Passage. We all have different anticipations and fears about this. Sailing across this piece of water scares the hell out of me. In my own mind, I can't get across this notorious passage quickly

enough. When I arrived in Ushuaia 17 days ago, I could not wait to head south, but the boat was still "out there," on its way across the Atlantic from Belgium. Frustrating to say the least. Six days into the wait and the wind has started blowing. Still having some gear to test, I head to the water to try out the kitesurfing equipment. Argentina has endless beaches of sand, rock and grass. I put a kite in the air and before long I'm kitesurfing in the Beagle Channel. The weather breaks and the sun comes out and all questions about my untested gear are answered. Despite the 40 degree water, I am toasty warm in my drysuit and with all systems working perfectly. I'm glad that I put considerable thought into preparing my gear for the extreme conditions. It could mean the difference between having a great time on the water and death. The quickly changing weather of this area is quite surprising, and a good reminder of the challenges yet to come.

27 December 2007 – At Sea/Drake Passage

What have I gotten myself into? The further into the Drake we get, the bigger the seas grow, and the more seasick I become. Outside on deck, I'm fine. But inside, I have to be horizontal or it feels like my head will explode and my insides will eject. The sounds of a boat in rough seas are so alien to me that it is difficult to get restful sleep. By early afternoon we are in 10-foot seas with 30-knot winds. Half-asleep, I suddenly hear an awful racket on deck. The Skipper races to see what is happening and finds the boom is broken into two pieces, with sail and rigging scattered all about. We're on a sailing expedition, so this can't be good. The Drake has taken its toll on not just us, but now our boat. Fortunately, we still have the jib sail and can continue south. Back inside, I lie down to fight the effect of the rolling ocean. We begin to call it the "horizontal club." I'm a charter member.

31 December 2007 – Davis Island

By early morning we're in Antarctic waters. I have spent the best part of the last five days in bed. Outside, it is extremely overcast and blowing, and although we have finally arrived, who cares, it's miserable out. After several hours of exploring, we find a spot to drop anchor. In an extremely tenuous moment, the wind pushes us onto an uncharted shoal. The sound of rock on the steel hull is horrifying! Rumen, the first mate, powers us through with the motor. Fortunately, on a second attempt at placing the anchor, it holds. We are all soberly reminded of the inherent dangers

Climbing ice, Antarctic style.   © Dixie Dansercoer

and extreme weather of this place. I can't believe the first night in Antarctica we ran aground. Thankfully no harm is done. With an auspicious start like this, there will certainly be no lack of excitement over the next several weeks.

4 January 2008 – Brabant Island

Fortunate experiences happen in life, but rarely are they of the kind that one will remember forever. Having already spent two birthdays in Antarctica, I never imagined spending yet another one on the ice. But in my 41st year, I get one more, and what a day! It started spectacularly in Buls Bay, anchored with icebergs, calving glaciers and mountains all around. We packed up our gear and journeyed to Brabant Island. Our plan: explore, climb, and experience the exact same places of the original Belgica crew. We ascend some rock outcroppings in order to recreate the historical photographs from 110 years ago. Precariously on a steep, glaciated slope, Dixie innocently says, "Hey, wait a minute.

We are forgetting something." And with that, the boys break into a chorus of "Happy Birthday," nearly bringing tears to my eyes. This is one birthday experience I will never forget. Tonight I fall asleep to the sound of whales breaching in the distance. Being the only one without a bunk below decks, I find it more comfortable to sleep outside, on deck when we are not underway. It's the perfect end to a perfect day.

5 January 2008 – Avicenna Bay, Brabant Island

Epic...no other way to describe today. After descending from Celsus Peak, our first real climb in Antarctica, we sail south in spectacular weather. I'm anxious to check out a small spit of land that I saw from the summit. My hopes are it will be a great spot for kitesurfing. We sail 45 minutes to Avicenna Bay, and the wind is perfect, as is the anchorage, the spot – everything! This narrow, rocky beach is the best we've seen for kiting. As I prepare my gear, I wonder what the half-dozen crab eater seals sunbathing, a stone's

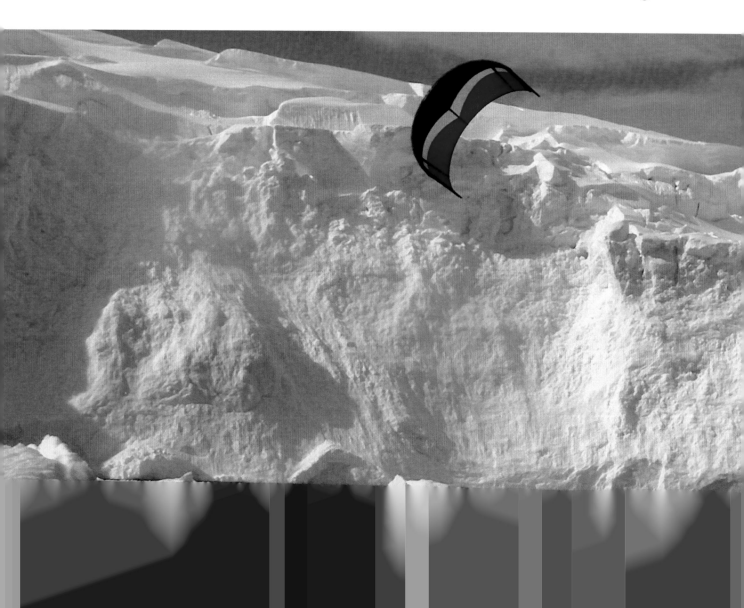

throw away, feel about our invasion on their turf. I triple-check everything before putting my kite in the air. In this environment, if something goes wrong, the consequences could be deadly. With that, I'm in the water and finally kitesurfing in Antarctica. It is wild and surreal! When I look around, I cannot believe the scenery. The Gerlache Strait is littered with icebergs of all sizes and the horizon is an endless mountain range. I'm blown away.

14 January 2008 – Arthur Harbor, Palmer Station

Today we stopped at Palmer Station, one of three U.S. scientific research bases in Antarctica. It was great to catch up with several friends whom I worked with at McMurdo years ago, that now spend their time at Palmer. Palmer is a nice place and has a certain small-town feel compared to the expansiveness of McMurdo. I must come back here one day and spend a season working and really explore this area. Oddly enough, the employees here are envious of our ability to leave the station and explore with the sailboat and we are envious of their cozy place they get to call home. We give a slide show of our expedition and everyone loves it. The reception afterwards and opportunity to get to know some of the people living here is a very special experience. And as always, Antarctica does not disappoint with low-angle sunlight turning the close-by glacier, orange, pink, and blue. Unreal.

15 January 2008 – False Cape Renard

Today we completed the historical aspect of our expedition, our 20th landing commemorating the original Belgica expedition. We believe that many of these places have not seen human visitors since Gerlache was here 110 years ago. It was interesting to set foot in the same places as the boys from the original Belgica. Between calving glaciers, strong currents, big waves, and extreme cold, each landing presented challenges none of us had anticipated. We took the

Gentoo penguins frolicking on the ice.
© Laurent Dick/www.sailantarctica.com

Kitesurfing along the Graham Coast.   © Laurent Dick/www.sailantarctica.com

same weather and temperature data and reshot the exact photos that Gerlache gathered. The findings show no conclusive evidence that anything has changed since 1897. Our entire crew expected otherwise and everyone was surprised at how little the ice and snow cover had changed from the historical photos.

19 January 2008 – Along the Graham Coast

The past few days have found us switching to a sailing-at-night schedule, headed due south to reach the Antarctic Circle. This is the part that becomes not so enjoyable for me. Two nights ago we spent countless hours in strong winds and high seas, travelling south. The minute this boat starts pitching and rolling I am seasick. Being a non-sailor, it is the one aspect of sailing life that I have not adjusted to. When the going gets tough, I have to be horizontal or outside on deck. Being seasick almost totally debilitates everything I am able to do.

After getting up at 4 in the morning, to help watch for ice in the water as Rumen drove us deeper south, I spent hours on deck trying to keep my composure and balance as the snow, wind, and sometimes rain made life on deck less than desirable. By Hour 2, I was even feeling seasick on deck. A few hours later, lying inside, hating life, I was ready to

get off at the next stop and never set foot on a sailing vessel again. Here is where the tradeoffs begin.

After we found a quiet anchor in a calm bay, I felt OK. Oh, and the wind was up, and well, I could probably go kitesurfing here and get back on the water! So, Rumen and I explore a small island only to get chased off by nesting Skua birds and a very curious leopard seal (who by the way are rumored to be quite dangerous, and are known to have killed one person in 2002.) The divers at Palmer told us they always get out of the water when there is a leopard seal in the area. Nonetheless, we explore some other small islands, only to end up back at the same island, with the kite in the air and me in the water. And, after being seasick for nearly 10 hours, I'm back on the water having the time of my life kiting past thousands of Adelie penguins, some on small islands, some on icebergs. Effortlessly weaving in and out of icebergs and at one point, even switching from kitesurfing to snowboarding as I hop up on a snow ramp on an iceberg and launch off. It is an unforgettable day. It is such a quandary to me that I can hate being on the water so much in a tiny sailing vessel and love being on the water behind a kite. It certainly is a world of tradeoffs. After several hours the wind dies down and I come across yet another, very large, leopard seal, who fortunately does not give chase. I think maybe I'm faster than him anyway. Thankfully, I kite away from the seal and back to the Belgica, anchored in a quiet, calm bay.

By midnight, we are sailing south again, and I'm horizontal wondering when the next bus stop will come, so I can get off this boat. And, the call goes out....WHALES! In one of those unforgettable moments, several minke whales start surfacing around the ship. And like none of us have ever seen before, begin playing in the wake of the bow. Playing like dolphins often do, rolling over, surfacing and having a grand time. P.J. calls these times, magic moments, and for this one, I would have to agree.

By 8:30 a.m. we are crossing the Antarctic Circle. We have to stop, just to savor the moment and have a toast. As so often happens, our thoughts turn to de Gerlache and his sailing crew 110 years ago, who crossed this same line, and pushed much deeper south. They were truly entering the unknown, unexplored realms of the Antarctic. We do the same in our own way, but with known maps and GPS. All of a sudden our thoughts are disrupted as the same two whales surface and start playing around the Belgica again. They have been following us for hours and put on another show to welcome us to the Antarctic Circle. And, I know, for right now, I love this place.

21-22 January 2008 – Hanusse Bay

Wild events transpired today. Well past the Antarctic Circle in Hanusse Bay, we hit pack ice that is too thick for the boat to get through. It stretches to the horizon. This is as far south as we will get this season. We drift, enjoying a free afternoon and spend the night, without much thought of the consequences. By morning we are hopelessly stuck in the ice, with no open water in sight. Overnight we have drifted further south and became stranded. Despite our efforts we cannot move and there is no choice but to let the ice decide our fate. Ironically, the original Belgica expedition became trapped in the pack ice as well, and as a result were forced to endure the first over-winter in Antarctica.

Concern among the crew is noticeable. Dixie sees our situation as dire and fears we could be stuck for weeks. My alarm is not so much getting out, but what could happen if one of the giant icebergs in the area moves with the current and hits the boat. The Skipper seems quite happy to be

The Belgica trapped in   © Laurent Dick/www.sailantarctica.com
ice near the Antarctic circle.

locked in the ice, and is prepared to hunker down for the winter. By nightfall, the wind and blinding snow are in full force, with big icebergs on the horizon approaching at an alarming rate. Rumen and I jump across ice flows to see how far we really are from open water. We climb an iceberg and see a channel that might offer an escape. The Skipper fires up the motor, and after 36 tenuous hours of being trapped in the ice, we are free and headed north. We've escaped, but now are sailing into the worst storm we've encountered. My watch, from 4 to 8 a.m., is the scariest experience I've had in years. After nearly colliding with big chunks of ice on more than one occasion due to lack of visibility, we are on full alert. Because of the rough seas, everyone is sick again. After 12 hours of misery, we find a safe anchorage in Stella Creek Bay. The strong winds and poor conditions continue. Nonetheless, the wind is blowing, so, right in front of Vernadsky Station, the only Ukrainian Station in Antarctica, I have a great time kiting amongst a dazzling array of icebergs.

January 2008 – Enterprise Island

I love this area. We are moored to an old whaling shipwreck that dates from the early 1900s. The rusting hull is a rare sign of human activity here. Despite the lousy weather, the wind is strong and steady. I launch my kite off a treacherous rocky cliff and kite out to some extraordinary icebergs towering several stories high, with huge arches

Having fun jumping between ice floes, © Laurent Dick/www.sailantarctica.com
while the Belgica is trapped in the ice.

eroded into their sides from constant wave bombardment. There is a big swell with rolling waves that provide great opportunities for jumping. I narrowly clear one giant berg with my kite and seconds later, two massive chunks calve off with a thunder. I absorb the resulting wave, but now there is so much ice in the water that I'm forced to leave the area to avoid disaster. The only way out is to tack behind another huge iceberg. But I don't anticipate its face being taller than my kite lines. The kite falls from the sky. I'm done. Thankfully, Rumen is there within minutes to retrieve me. Today was just absolutely out of control!

29 January 2008 – The Drake Shake

After a month in Antarctica, it is finally time to head north, back to Ushuaia. I'm not thrilled about crossing the Drake again, because it seems that a rolling ship and I don't agree. I have some serious concerns about the five-day crossing, but we have a decent weather forecast and despite the threat of a raging storm that may or may not intersect our path, the Skipper forges ahead. I have no interest in experiencing 30-foot seas in this lifetime, but it seems we are going to roll the dice again and make our way across the Drake. Within hours, I'm seasick and horizontal below decks watching waves wash over the deck from the window above my head. By Day 4, I am in a constant state of alert as our 47-foot boat is pitched around like a cork. I am certain that we will roll over and capsize at any moment. For 16 hours, we are hammered by 15-foot seas. I swear that if I get back alive, I'll never set foot on a boat again. Oddly enough, the storm stalls, and the last day is calm for the sail up the Beagle Channel, back to Ushuaia. By morning, a full blown gale is raking the Beagle and northern sections of the Drake. A cruise ship battling the storm reports gusts of 100 miles per hour. I don't even want to imagine what kind of roller coaster that must be.

3 February 2008 – Back to the Real World

Mixed emotions surround the team's final days together in Ushuaia. In my experience, intense expeditions usually end with elation and sadness all at the same time. We stay busy in an effort to keep our minds off the inevitable

Icebergs along the Antarctic Peninsula.

© Laurent Dick/www.sailantarctica.com

goodbyes. We have endured hardships and fears not found in our normal, daily lives. And in the end, we had only each other to rely on for support.

I'm one of the last to leave as the team departs Ushuaia, one after another, and I feel a bittersweet crush of emotions. This has been the expedition of a lifetime. For me, it didn't start out as a kitesurfing trip, but that is what it turned into. I had the opportunity to experience some of the most extreme and remarkable kitesurfing of my life. In some respects, kitesurfing in Antarctica was just like any other day in the water. Riding under the kite, feeling the wind – it felt the same. But then, I'd look around and just shake my head in awe at the magnitude and beauty of my surroundings. I guess in some ways, being the first one to ever kite in Antarctic waters parallels what Gerlache and his crew achieved 110 years ago. Not just exploring geographic boundaries, but exploring the potential of what humans can do in an extreme environment. This has been one of the most intense and emotionally touching experiences of my life. With a heavy heart I head for home.

L-R: Michel Tordoir, Laurent Dick, Troy, Frans Doomen,
Pieterjan Kempynck, Rumen Grozev, Dixie Dansercoer.
The Belgica Expedition team on Peterman Island.

© *Laurent Dick/www.sailantarctica.com*

The Stats:

Meters of kites on board – 42

Meters of sails on board – 115

Weight of ship – 15 tons

Pounds of rice consumed – 85

Pounds of pasta consumed – 65

Number hours of video footage from trip – 60

Number of photographs from the trip – 15,000

Number of hours spent seasick – 216

Number of hours spent kiting – 10

Number of kitesurf sessions in Antarctica – 6

Number of kitesurf sessions in Ushuaia – 6

Number of days spent on land – 4

Number of days spent on board – 38

Number of days slept on deck – 22

Number of days in Antarctic waters – 30

Number of days on the Drake Passage - 10

Number of days spent in Ushuaia before and after expedition - 30

Number of days off work for expedition – 90

Number of days I really missed not being at work – 0

Heading into the Yukon.

© Troy Henkels

CHAPTER TWENTY-TWO

ALONE ALONG THE ALCAN

Riding a motorcycle on long, open roads has always appealed to me. I suppose it's the freedom or maybe the opportunity to think and reflect as the miles roll past. My time on the road always keeps me anticipating that next road trip.

My plan was to drive from my front door in Alaska to my Dad's front door in Iowa. It's about 3,600 miles one way, and I had a week to do it. Fall seemed like the best time to avoid RV and tourist traffic on the Alcan (Alaska/Canadian Highway) and still utilize the relative long daylight hours of the Far North. And of course, it's wise to get out of Alaska before it gets too cold for motorbiking.

On a Friday in late August I load everything necessary for a week-long journey across the open roads of Alaska, Canada, and the lower 48 States. My plan is to camp the

entire trip, pack my own food, and not buy a thing except fuel. After work, I head east from Eagle River, through some of the most beautiful mountains in the state. As the sun sets, I watch the Wrangell-St. Elias mountains light up on the southern horizon. I ride the first 310 miles to Tok, Alaska, arriving just as darkness is setting in. The sound of geese, far overhead, beating their way south, lull me to sleep.

I am on the road again before sunrise. With temperatures in the 40s, it makes for some chilly riding well into mid-day. The road crews are out in full force, trying to get their work done before freeze-up. Just when I think I am making good time, I am stopped for a construction zone, seemingly in the middle of nowhere. For whatever reasons, the Alaskan and Canadian governments feel this road in this particular area needs repair. At several stops, I wait for over a half-hour. As I pass the large machinery repairing pavement, I can't help but see the wheels of progress working against a vast wilderness. Fortunately, in these parts, the wilderness is still winning the battle.

I almost collide with several buffalo, first with a solo beast near the road and, later, with a herd of 20 running parallel to the road. Taking out one of these with a motorbike would not be a good option, so I am happy to get past them with just a close call. At a gas stop, I meet another solo motorcyclist heading south – a guy in his 20s who was sticking to the speed limit after he had gotten a ticket just outside of Tok. He had been running at 140 m.p.h. but had slowed to 80 when the trooper pulled him over. He told me his bike can do 189 m.p.h. and I have no doubt how he knows this. Just after dark and in the pouring rain, I pull into a welcome spot, Liard Hot Springs. Having driven this highway 13 times already, I knew of this haven of hot water in the middle of the woods. After a long soak, I hunker down for the night.

Having just arrived from Alaska, Dad (left) and his buddy Harold tell me I'm crazy.   © Troy Henkels

The next day, after several hundred miles of spectacular landscape, I arrive in Dawson Creek, the start/finish of the Alaska Highway. Across Canada, I decide to stay as far north as possible, on roads I had never traveled before. As the miles roll beneath me and I work my way east, the more it feels like home. This is farm country. I pass mile after mile of fenceless wheat fields that stretch to the horizon. For hour after hour, I see no other vehicle. I suspect there are not too many places left on this planet where you can do this. By sunset and with 800 miles behind me for the day, I find a spectacular spot on Lesser Great Slave Lake and roll out my sleeping bag. This night I sleep under the stars. I can't remember when I'd been somewhere where it was this dark and had so many stars out.

I awaken to frost on my sleeping bag, and I ride for several hours with ice on my jacket and bike. It warms up by late morning, and I am determined to make it as close to Lake Winnipeg as I can. On a map, the road between Lake Winnipeg, Lake Winnipegosis, and Lake Manitoba looks like a motorcyclist's dream: a long stretch of lone highway cutting through pristine wilderness.

Before I reached this stretch of road, I had asked people in every town what it was like up that highway. Amazingly, no one had ever been up there. One guy even told me that I was just asking for trouble by going there.

I wind up driving that road in a driving rain, and it is one time in my life that I realize I have made a poor decision. It's not that it isn't a fine road, but the pouring rain, lack of scenic pullouts, and kamikaze truckers make for an exciting and somewhat precarious driving experience. By nightfall, I am in Minneapolis, staying with my old friend Jody, with whom I had been in Boy Scouts back in Iowa. Sometimes, keeping up with your past is the best way to keep perspective on your present.

The next morning I ride south from Minneapolis on the Great River Road, passing through Red Wing, Winona, La Crosse, and Guttenberg. Though I am relatively close to home, there are sections of this road I have never traveled. It is some of the most scenic landscape on the entire trip.

After five days on the road and 3,660 miles, I pull into my Dad's driveway in Dubuque. As my Dad and his lifelong friend Harold ask me about the trip, I realize that I have just connected my present with my past, by one long motorcycle ride. The best part of this trip, like every other grand adventure, is coming home.

Getting ready to descend into Ram Valley.　　　　　　　　　　　　　© Troy Henkels

CHAPTER TWENTY-THREE

A LONG DAY OUT

One of the things I enjoy the most about living in Alaska is exploring mountain ranges and backcountry that few people ever experience. Alaska is so vast that it is easy to get off the beaten path and feel like you are setting foot in a wilderness paradise for the first time.

Even though I have had some amazing opportunities to explore some of the most remote corners of the planet, one of my favorite activities is to hike right from my home in Eagle River, Alaska. In my current life of gear-intensive extreme expeditions, it's a treat to be able to walk out the door with a day pack and a few provisions. For several summers I have been eyeing a long mountain ridge that goes deep into the Chugach Mountain Range. I haven't been able to find anyone who could tell me much about the ridge line, peaks,

and mountain valleys within the Peters Creek drainage. As a result, these several unknowns increased its appeal for me.

After poring over topographical maps, I chose one ridgeline to hike and several valleys to explore and figured the mileage would be 20 to 30 miles. By any standard, that is a long day in the mountains. Considering the unknowns in terrain, river crossings, and mountain passes I didn't really know how long it would take or how difficult this hike would be. For one of the first times in recent memory, I wondered and doubted if I had the endurance to complete this grueling hike in a day's time. Having turned 40 several years ago, I know that my muscles and body certainly can't do what they did when I was 20. And, judging from the topo maps, even if I were still 20, this would be an extremely grueling hike.

165

Giant fireweed and a few monkshood in the Peters Creek Valley.

© Troy Henkels

On an overcast Saturday, I load my daypack and hit the trail early. The weather looks tenuous at best and the cool temperatures seem to indicate a storm brewing. The initial climb up Bear Mountain to access the ridge takes about an hour on good trail. Once on top of the mountain, I start to connect a long ridge line that goes from peak to peak to peak, running deep into the mountains. For hours, I hike up one mountain and then down the backside of the same peak before having to start up the next mountain. This entire ridge is riddled with a series of smaller peaks that drive me toward larger peaks farther into the mountain range. The views from this ridgeline are stunning in all directions, offering a perspective on these mountains that I have not seen before.

After four hours traversing this ridge, I reach the high peaks just as a storm front is working its way down the glacier at the head of the valley. I hope to climb for another hour and hit three more of these bigger peaks before descending into the valley. My hopes are dashed when rain starts to pelt my Gore-Tex jacket, and clouds obscure the final two peaks.

I descend into Peters Creek Valley via a sharp ridge line that dropped all the way to the valley floor. Halfway down the ridge, I notice two black dots directly in my path far below – obviously wildlife of some sort and a good chance that they are black bears, which are abundant in this area. Being too far away to really tell and now into alders over my head, I decide to hike straight at whatever they are. Despite the danger, I reason that if they are two bears they will smell me and take off. If they don't, well I'll worry about that when the time comes. If they are moose, no problem; they pose little threat in the wilderness. By the time I bushwhack the last quarter-mile to reach the valley floor, I miss the wildlife by a hundred yards. The dots are two big moose that don't seem to mind my meanderings one bit.

Wading through a meadow of dense five-foot wildflowers, I feel something underfoot. I have come across an overgrown hunting trail. I decide to use this "trail" to lead me farther up the valley toward even more remote territory. This will allow me to climb out of the valley and into an alpine bowl that I had hoped to reach, had I not been forced off that initial ridgeline by procellous weather. It is pouring rain as I hike through dense undergrowth and constantly watch for bears. Because of the dense vegetation I can't actually see the trail; I am more or less hiking by "feel." After several hours, near the head of the valley and the Peters Glacier, I start climbing out of the valley

167

The long ridge that led me deep into the Chugach mountains.

© Troy Henkels

and up into the mountains opposite the ridgeline I descended several hours earlier. Before doing this, I must fjord Peters Creek, which is running fast and furious due to a torrent of rain the week before. After a brief break, I traverse the thigh-deep, frigid water without incident and start climbing into one of the most beautiful mountain valleys I have ever experienced.

The peaks on this side of the valley are much more severe than on the other. They offer vertical rocky cliffs that soar nearly 5,000 feet above me. As the valley curves deeper into the mountains, I continue to climb. The terrain ranges from alpine tundra to rocks the size of houses that have avalanched off the mountain faces and swept across the entire valley floor. Finally, standing on top of the mountain pass and looking into the next valley, I find myself perplexed and daunted as I peer nearly vertically down the cliff face that I must descend. There is no easy way down, particularly on wet rock. But I know from experience in the mountains that I can find a way if I just try. Sure enough, before long I come across a somewhat precarious sheep trail that skirts diagonally across the cliff, all the way to the valley floor.

I slowly descend and am grateful to finally be down safe and in another beautiful alpine valley. I quickly notice I am not alone. There are sheep all over the cliffs and valley floor – more than 50 in this one valley.

With my head down and rain pelting my back, I trudge up the next steep mountain pass that will lead me out of the mountains. I am relieved to hit the top and look down into Ram Valley and Eagle River Valley – the route back home. This descent is steep, but not as daunting as the last vertical descent. Once in Ram Valley, I hiked on glacier scree all the way out of the valley. This eventually takes me back down to tree line and into the alders of Eagle River Valley. On sore legs and now racing darkness, I make it back to civilization safely.

Despite my apprehensions I have pulled it off. Having been on the go for 14 hours and covering nearly 25 miles of some pretty severe mountain wilderness, I am tired. My muscles ache and I am wet to the bone. But overall I am relieved that my body is still able to do what I ask it to do in the Alaska wilderness.

CHAPTER TWENTY-FOUR

THE NORTH BOUND QUEST

All I can do is to try to focus on staying warm. My fingers are so dangerously cold, that if I think about anything other than warming them up, they will become frostbitten. Nonetheless, it is more important to tend to several others in the group who are obviously struggling more than me. Plus, I must get the camera rolling to capture footage of this team and their quest; that is my job. So, like I have so many times on this trip already, I take care of everything else first and then work on bringing my fingers back to life, before it is too late.

The North Bound Quest Team in Longyearbyen, Spitsbergen prior to our departure.

© Troy Henkels

This expedition is like no other that I have been on. At the request of my longtime expedition partner Dixie Dansercoer, I am helping him guide 10 business professionals and three doctors on an expedition to ski the last degree to the North Pole. There are 11 Dutch and Belgians and two Americans. Although the distance is not that great – only 60 miles – there is an array of other factors that will make this expedition an extreme challenge.

I can handle the cold and the guiding, but I have been asked to be the cinematographer, recording video for a

documentary. This I can do as well, but I have never balanced guiding and filming in such harsh conditions as the Arctic Ocean.

Although somewhat inexperienced in cold weather and polar travel, the North Bound Quest team had, a year earlier, prepared with a week-long expedition crossing a large ice field in Iceland. They also underwent a full year of serious physical training, mostly involving long treks in the woods and sand dunes, dragging old tires around to replicate the dragging of a sled. This not only provided good physical conditioning, it was good mental training as it replicated the sometimes frustrating work of dragging a sled through chaotic ice.

In April, the team assembles in Longyearbyen, Spitsbergen, a remote island off the coast of Norway in the North Atlantic. This is the stepping-off point for many North Pole expeditions. For four days, the team meticulously organizes and packs the necessary food and gear. We have several logistics meetings with the Russians, as they will fly us to our drop-off point and offer support if we have

Loading the Russian Mi 8 helicopter.

© Troy Henkels

problems. There is an afternoon venturing onto the sea ice around Spitsbergen to get the team acclimatized to pulling heavy sleds through variable ice conditions in the extreme cold.

With quiet excitement and a lot of anticipation we board a Russian Antonov 72 airplane destined for Barneo, an even more remote outpost. Barneo is a base set up on the sea ice by the Russians to assist expeditions, scientists, and tourists wanting to experience the Arctic Ocean and North Pole regions. Every spring, the Russians go to great lengths and expense to set up a base on the sea ice for only a month of activity. Our stay at Barneo is short – just enough to realize it's really cold out (minus-22F/minus-30C), to acquire fuel, and to pack two shotguns in case of polar bear encounters. We then cram (and I mean cram) into a helicopter for the flight to our starting point. The Russian Mi 8 chopper is bigger, louder, and looks more dangerous than anything I

have ever flown in. Just the thought of this thing being able to get off the ground is a bit unsettling. We have an all-Russian crew, and I watch the pilots calmly smoke cigarettes as we lift off in a whirlwind of spindrift. The 20-minute ride is deafening. It takes us over an endless array of sea ice, open leads, and pressure ridges, before dropping us off exactly one degree from the North Pole (89'N and 13'E, to be exact). The helicopter disappears over the horizon and the sound fades to create total silence. We are alone on the ice. The magnitude of our situation sets in.

We stand on a thin layer of sea ice suspended over 4,000 feet of Arctic Ocean. It is calm and clear and minus-31F/minus-35C. Despite the cold, the team enthusiastically and intuitively begins what we have come here to do. Harnesses get clipped to sleds, skis snapped into bindings, and everyone falls in line behind Dixie as he starts skiing north. It's a sudden and extreme change to this new environment, but it is what we have all been waiting for. With time, the team will acclimate to the cold and the 150-pound sleds. In these temperatures you really have to keep moving or you become dangerously cold quite quickly. My fingers are close to becoming frostbitten as I help the last of the group with final adjustments and film the departure. Then I get moving and start to bring my fingers back to life.

Traveling conditions on the Arctic Ocean are quite variable at this time of year. It is a chaotic, flat landscape of broken-up sea ice for as far as you can see in all directions. The opposing forces of nature at work here are powerful and intense. Pressure from opposing currents and wind heave blocks of sea ice onto piles as big as houses. Our challenge is to navigate these as directly and efficiently as possible and keep moving north toward the Pole. Sometimes this is easy and other times it seems impossible. Open water is particularly challenging, as is ice that is on the move and colliding and separating right in front of our eyes.

At the end of the first day, we camp on a relatively safe section of flat "old" ice between a variety of pressure ridges and jumbled ice blocks. At this latitude, at this time of year, there is no night. It is impossible to tell night from day, as there is sunlight 24 hours a day. Our goal is to cover eight to 10 miles a day and, in a week's time, reach the Pole. This is a challenging prospect, considering the movement and nature of a very fickle Arctic Ocean.

Fortunately, our team operates flawlessly. We expect the first few days to be an adjustment period for a group that has largely never camped or traveled in extreme cold. Every night there are many repairs to be made; at these temperatures, the equipment is susceptible to breaking. In polar environments, there is little

room for wasting energy and not being prepared. Everyone has learned the importance of getting into routines when traveling. If you can learn how to manage the cold and your body, so you do not freeze extremities, it is possible to exist in this environment, be comfortable, and have fun.

Day 2 is perfect traveling weather: sunny with no wind. The ice conditions are variable, with some long stretches of flat ice interspersed with navigating pressure ridges made up of piles of ice blocks the size of garages. These are not only challenging but also time-consuming for a large group like ours to negotiate. Despite the cold, we make good time. After a long but beautiful day, we cover nearly eight miles. It is minus-22F/ minus-30C, and once we stop it is a race to set up camp; change into dry and warm clothes, get a stove going to melt snow for water, and make food. The team has done this over and over again, but no amount of practice can prepare you for what it feels like to be traveling and living on the Arctic Ocean in these temperatures.

Everyone on the team will remember this particular night. Shortly after setting up camp, Joost, the leader and strongest in the group, cannot seem to warm up his fingers.

The NBQ team working together to negotiate difficult ice en route to the North Pole.

© Troy Henkels

Dixie works to warm them up, but he soon realizes that the fingers are like blocks of wood. Severe frostbite. The erstwhile leader of the group is reduced to tears by the realization that his fingers might have to be amputated. His expedition is over. Dixie places the satellite phone call to the Russians and Joost is soon evacuated by helicopter. The dangerous reality of this environment and expedition hit home with everyone on the team as they stand shivering and watch their leader, motivator, and muse disappear over the horizon back to an uncertain future.

By morning, everyone is struggling to stay warm. Even me. It's minus-26F/minus-32C and getting colder. I had anticipated it warming up and so dressed too lightly. Partway through filming the team, I must stop and add a layer of fleece and try to warm up. It literally takes me hours to warm up my hands to the point where I feel comfortable again. Nonetheless, the landscape is ever-changing and nothing short of spectacular. The pressure ridges and compression zones on the Arctic Ocean offer some of the most amazing and chaotic piles of blue ice anywhere.

After covering 8½ miles, we set up camp. The wind has been building, amplifying the cold, but everyone on the team is doing well. Before long I am summoned to the tent of our only married couple on the trip, Ruud and Sabine. Despite already being in the tent for nearly an hour, one of Sabine's fingers is frostbitten and another is frost-nipped. She is nearly hypothermic. Ruud is so exhausted that there is little he can do to help her. I pour all the energy I have into these two people. I retrieve my hot liquids and immediately get warm water and food into them. By massaging Sabine's nearly frozen hands, feet, and body, I hope to warm her up and bring her fingers back to life. Another call goes out to the Russians for a medivac. They say they can possibly come in the morning. My journal entry for this day starts with, "Today was a brutal journey."

In the morning, the Russians inform us that Sabine's frostbite is not severe enough for a medivac – even though they haven't seen it. She will have to endure and make it through until we are picked up at the Pole. She is devastated and demoralized. Nonetheless, the team pitches in to help get Sabine and Ruud packed up and into the skis for another day of pulling the sleds north. Within an hour, Sabine goes

from devastation to being on top of the world. She is ecstatic to be back on her skis and moving. Although still in pain, she has a great day and is thrilled that she was forced to remain on the ice. To see this transformation over such a short period is something that I will never forget.

Throughout Day 4 we watch the weather deteriorate. The wind picks up. The skies become overcast, making the light flat, which in turn makes it difficult to see and navigate effectively. Fortunately, as the bad weather moves in, the temperature rises and this makes things easier to deal with. Despite the poor visibility and strong wind, we continue heading north. Fortunately, the wind is always at our sides or backs. We are able to cover 7½ miles.

Every morning and every night, we use the GPS to make a careful calculation of our mileage for the day and how much distance we lost or gained due to the drift of the ice pack. We announce our findings to the team. Because we are on the ocean and there is current, we stand to lose or gain mileage overnight depending on that drift. Unfortunately for us, all too often we experience negative drift. This means, despite always making mileage north during the day, overnight we lose some (or all) of that mileage due to the southerly drift.

On Day 5, the wind has really picked up and the light is incredibly flat. It's monochromatic and miserable. We travel for eight hours, make nine miles, and quickly set up camp amid deteriorating conditions. By the time all are in their tents, we are in a full-blown blizzard. Ferocious wind and blowing snow hammers us all night long. The storm rages on in the morning, when we awaken to find our tents half-buried and sleds totally buried. We recognize that we won't be going anywhere until the wind subsides. What's more, we look at the GPS and realize that for the second day in a row, we have lost all the mileage we gained from the previous day's travel. This deals a serious blow to the group's psyche. We are on a big treadmill called the Arctic Ocean.

The storm breaks by the afternoon and we pack up and resume heading north. No one is interested in giving up the dream to reach the North Pole. The temperatures have warmed up to an amazing 32F/0C. We come across our first open water. However, a short time later, the weather deteriorates rapidly and the wind returns. We are immersed in a dangerous maze of pressure ridges, ice blocks, and open water. Dixie excels in these conditions, and he sniffs out a safe passage. We set up camp during a total whiteout after covering less than three miles. In communication with Barneo, the Russians tell us that they will pull us off the ice in two days. The negative drift and bad weather are too much for us to overcome. The realization comes into focus that there is no way that we will make it to the North Pole this season. It's difficult news for the team, but on the Arctic Ocean there are things that cannot be controlled. Reality can be a bitter pill.

We only cover three miles on our seventh day, but it really doesn't matter. The negative drift takes away all mileage that we gain. Still, the team is in surprisingly good spirits and still enjoying this polar environment. The traveling today consists of an endless maze of stunning blue ice blocks and pressure ridges. We find a nice area of open water and break out special drysuits that Dixie and I packed so that everyone can have a swim in the ocean. It is a huge morale-booster and always fun to swim amidst ice and snow.

When we camp that night, everyone gathers in one of the bigger tents for a fun night of stories and enjoying the moment. As the storm continues outside, the team savors every moment together and the time we still have on the ice. The expedition will be over soon, yet no one is quite ready

for it to end. The weather is too severe for travel the next day, and we continue to lose distance due to the southerly drift.

By late afternoon, however, the sky clears and the sun comes out. Everyone enjoys the break in the weather and the chance to dig out tents and sleds that the storm had buried. The wind is still blowing, so I waste no time to seize the rare opportunity to put a kite in the air. I kite-ski for miles, enjoying the Arctic Ocean in all its grandeur. The kiting is spectacular, and I venture as far from camp as I dare without getting lost.

The swoop of the rotors signals us that the Russian helicopter has arrived to take us off the ice. We pack up and cram (and I mean cram) into the helicopter. We are soon airborne and looking down on the chaos of ice that we were a part of for the past eight days. While peering out the helicopter window, I have mixed feelings. I'm sad to go, but happy to leave.

The Russians fly us north, to 90 degrees north, and land at the geographic North Pole. Our team has about 30 minutes to savor the feeling of actually standing at the top of the world. Everyone is thrilled, despite not having made it here under our own power. For me, it was dream come true. As I look out across an endless landscape of snow and ice, there are only two things that I want to do. The first is

Snowkiting on the Arctic Ocean.

to call my Father back in Iowa. I had called him from the South Pole several years earlier, and now I really want to call him from the North Pole. With the advent of the satellite phone, it has been a thrill to share my expeditions with him by calling from some pretty remote places. He answers on the first ring. It has never felt better to hear his voice than while standing on the Arctic Ocean. After the call, I grabbed my boomerang. Standing on the North Pole, I threw that boomerang around the world. I suspect that I'm the first – and probably only one ever – to throw a boomerang around the world from both the North and South poles.

All too soon the deafening sound of the helicopter is heard on the horizon. We load up, fly back to Barneo, board the Antonov 72, and land back in Spitsbergen a few hours later, expedition complete. Everyone suddenly finds themselves awkwardly adjusting from life on the Arctic Ocean, back to civilization and creature comforts. The end of an expedition and this transition is always a bittersweet experience.

At our final team dinner, before everyone departs for families, jobs, and reality, I'm amazed by the perspective that this expedition has provided. Despite the fact that we were not able to make it to the Pole under our own power, it is a very special and deeply moving experience for each of us. The lessons learned and the opportunity to step so far out of normal life and a regular comfort zone make an impact and provide memories that will last a lifetime.

Throwing a boomerang around the world at the North Pole.   © Dixie Dansercoer

For me, the lessons from this expedition are clear. It's important to appreciate every moment and experience, for what it is, rather than focusing directly on the goal and the impending success or failure. Nothing in life ever goes as planned. This much I believe to be true, whether in real life or trying to reach the North Pole under adverse conditions. The biggest thing is this: Always mind your fingers and do everything you can to keep them warm.

Postscript: Frostbite took its toll on the fingers of Joost and Sabine, but neither required amputation. Although a painful process, they have more or less recovered from their injuries. Neither has full feeling back in the fingers, and in cold weather they still experience pain in the fingertips. Fortunately, I never experienced frostbite during my time on the Arctic Ocean, despite being dangerously close on several occasions. The footage and story I captured on film was intended for a documentary on Discovery Channel and for a TV show in Europe. It wound up in a documentary that received limited distribution, "The Northbound Quest…Walking the Last Degree." It provides good memories for the expedition team. To date, I have still heard of no one that has thrown boomerangs around the world at the North and South poles. And I still wonder how my Father knows how important it is to me, for him to be home when I call from remote corners of the planet. I have yet to get his answering machine.

174

CHAPTER TWENTY-FIVE

ANOTHER DATE WITH THE STRAIT

Geared up and ready to cross the Strait.   © Bjorn Detre

Standing on the westernmost point of North America is daunting. Looking across and contemplating crossing this precarious stretch of water using kites, in summertime, is mind-boggling. I had first thought about Kitesurfing across the Bering Strait in the winter of 2005, when Dixie and I attempted to walk across to Russia. At one point on that crossing, I put a kite in the air but wasn't able to make much progress. The sea ice was so broken up, it was obvious that kites were not a practical means of travel in winter. Then it

occurred to me that summer would be the time to attempt a crossing using kites.

When Geza Scholtz found me through the Internet and asked if it were possible to kitesurf across the Strait, I was quick to reply. It was absolutely possible, but I also knew it would be a time-consuming expedition to plan and an expensive one at that. Swiss-born, Geza was well traveled, and like me, an extremely active kiter. We both had been kitesurfing in various places around the world for the better part of 10 years. Our common passion for this sport made us an ideal team to attempt be the first to accomplish this.

The challenges and dangers of attempting such an endeavor are far-ranging, but possibly the biggest is negotiating the labyrinth of insane logistics required for an expedition on the Strait. If we could manage that, the actual kiting across would seem like the easy part. An expedition in this part of the world poses plenty of challenges, and we had to be prepared for the worst: cold water (40F), strong currents, and some of the most severe and unpredictable weather anywhere. And, of course, the scary and very real possibility of being stranded in the middle of the Strait, where a rescue might be days away. Nonetheless, a relatively warm weather expedition sounded inviting, and I was itching to see the Strait in summertime.

By far, the biggest difficulty was securing the proper permits to enter Russia legally. We discussed at great lengths making a crossing without Russian permits. Not only did we decide this was somewhat irresponsible, but our sponsors would not endorse such a plan. Plus, I was not real anxious to spend any time in a Russian jail. Since we would be using the wind for our crossing, we didn't know exactly where we would land if we actually made it across. There are no official border stations near the Russian side of the Strait, so it was an issue with the Russians to get a permit to enter at an unofficial border crossing. After eight months of trying to secure the proper permits, our liaison in Russia disappeared. Well, he quit corresponding with us after we were assured we were close to having the permits in hand. Only three months away from our scheduled departure date and confronted with some major roadblocks, it seemed possible that we would not begin the expedition as scheduled. We had to start the permit process all over, knowing it was a complex and time-consuming process with no guarantee of success. Finally, a Moscow-based PR agency that represented our biggest sponsor stepped in and was able to push our permits through in the nick of time. The Russians, always full of tenacity, said the permits would cost $70,000 to $100,000! When we heard this, Geza and I started scrambling for cash and more sponsors. After all was said and done, we paid $45,000, which was still a staggering sum just for permission to kite 56 miles. Astounded by the year of chaos, expense, effort, and frustration in dealing with the Russians, we were now officially cleared to kitesurf across the Bering Strait.

We headed for Wales, Alaska, the westernmost point on the North American continent and the closest point to Russia. It is a remote native village of 150 residents, most of whom don't have running water or toilets. Wales sits on a desolate beach surrounded inland by great expanses of marshy tundra and mountains. On a clear day, you actually can see Russia. Several geographical features come together here to create extreme ocean currents, unpredictable seas, and wind and weather that change very quickly. From experience, I knew that just showing up at the Bering Strait was no guarantee that we would be able to make it across to Russia. Our only hope was that we'd be able to pull it off with a little perseverance, hard work, and luck.

Before we could actually start an attempt, we needed a dependable support boat. There aren't a lot of boats in this part of the world, and none that was willing to support our expedition. The locals use their boats for subsistence, and summer is the time for fishing. So we had to buy a boat in Anchorage, disassemble it, ship it to Nome, and reassemble it. Then we trailered it to Teller (another native village on the coast), put it in the water and drove it 60 miles up the coast to Wales. This was a small adventure in itself, and just this took our support team two weeks to accomplish. The biggest problem occurred on the last leg, on the way to Wales. A two-hour trip turned into an eight-hour ordeal, after one of the engines suddenly stopped working. The team was a little rattled by this experience in the open ocean, but they were able to limp into Wales after dark, safe and without further incident.

This 20-foot Zodiac should have been the perfect support craft. But it was fraught with engine problems, and in the first week of the expedition it became apparent that this boat was a liability rather than the safety tool it was supposed to be. The boat proved to be the biggest point of frustration in the entire expedition. We watched several perfect wind days come and go while we were grounded on the beach wrenching on the Zodiac. When we finally had

L-R: Bjorn Detre, Andre Scholtz, Geza Scholtz, Andor Scholtz, Troy, Laurent Bobay. The Bering Strait team.

© Troy Henkels

176

Kitesurfing on the Bering Strait in Wales, Alaska. Those are whale bones in the foreground.

© Bjorn Detre

all the Zodiac issues worked out, we made an attempt, but had to return to shore, not once but twice, because of engine problems. Our frustrations had hit an all-time high, and we sat down that night to discuss a new game plan.

We decided to sell the boat and hire Ronald, a local boat captain from Little Diomede who had a 20-foot fiberglass skiff with an 80-horsepower engine. That would be more than adequate for a support boat. Ronald grew up and lives on Little Diomede, an Alaskan island village sitting right in the middle of the Strait. Ronald knew the Bering Strait well. He shared many stories about his polar bear hunts on sea ice in winter and walrus- and whale-hunting trips in the summer. We were confident that he and his boat would be well-suited to serve us in a support role.

Surprisingly, several days of absolutely perfect wind passed, with Ronald saying "no way" to venturing out into

rough seas with his boat. The locals have a healthy respect for the weather and ocean on the Strait, and they know the dangers of being caught out in building storms and seas. The thought of being capsized in big swells will keep even an experienced captain on shore. Despite the lack of a support boat, we still ventured out onto the Bering Strait for some epic kiting sessions in great surf and perfect wind. After one five-hour day on the water, venturing far out into the main current and big rollers, my GPS indicated that I had done 60 miles! This was the same mileage it would take to get across the entire Strait. But I wasn't in Russia; I was still in Wales. This assured both of us that actually crossing the Strait was within reason.

On our first day kiting, it soon became clear that the survival gear we planned on carrying would take some getting used to. It was necessary that we be equipped for any

177

Kitesurfing on the Bering Strait.

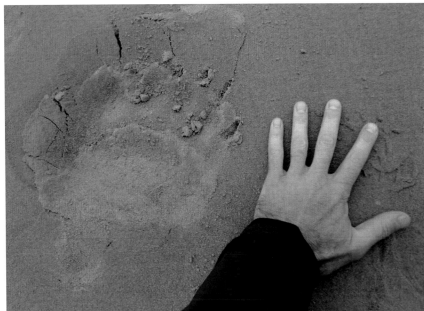

Polar bear tracks.   © Troy Henkels

© Bjorn Detre

emergency. In addition to our boards and kites, we had full drysuits, helmets, lifejackets, food, water, flares, air horn and Spot trackers. We planned for the worst and, considering the boat issues we'd already experienced, I had my concerns about being stranded in the middle of the Strait without a boat.

Despite the typical dismal weather, the locals told us that August this year had an uncommon number of no-wind days. With nothing left to do but wait, we enjoyed the local culture and community as much as we could. Some of the highlights were Eskimo baseball on Main Street with just about every kid in the village. Basketball in the school gym with the older kids and adults. We even got to explore an abandoned Cold War-era radar site named White Alice, in the mountains behind Wales. Several afternoons were spent on the beach helping our host Dan cut driftwood into firewood. The hardy locals were not only friendly, but extremely curious about our project. Their help was invaluable, particularly during the early stages of the expedition.

The most memorable day found our cameraman Bjorn and me hiking along the beach when we spotted a polar bear ahead in the distance. Bjorn immediately started to run toward the bear for a closer look and better pictures. It has never seemed prudent to me to run AT a bear, so I convinced him of a more subtle and slower approach. As we got closer, the bear lumbered across the beach, crawled into the ocean, and swam off, never to be seen again.

The most surprising element of the Bering Strait – and biggest concern for our team – is the wild weather. You can experience all four seasons in less than an hour. We would have to rely on a consistent wind to take us the full distance to Russia. If the wind changes partway across, it could mean stalling our kites, or finding ourselves in perilous danger, confronting overpowering winds and building, turbulent seas. We were searching for a fine line of a steady, strong wind (20 knots), and fairly calm seas to allow a safe passage for not only the kiters, but also our support boat.

Finally, after patient anticipation, we had one day that offered the perfect conditions to attempt a crossing.

The wind was blowing and the seas were calm. Ronald fired up the boat, and we donned our gear and launched our kites. We kited away from Wales and watched the edge of North America fall away in the distance. Just when it was looking like we might make it to Russia, the wind died and our kites fell from the sky. With a mixture of frustration and awe, we climbed aboard our support boat and returned to Wales.

After a year of planning, countless logistical nightmares, three weeks in Wales, and fall storms imminent, we had to abandon our efforts to get across. For me, there was no disappointment in not making the crossing. From years of seemingly unsuccessful expeditions, I have learned that nothing ever goes as planned and big goals can often be elusive. The reward is not so much in reaching the destination, but how much you enjoy the journey. And this one turned out to be the journey of a lifetime.

Sunset on the Bering Strait. Diomede Islands (left) and Russia (right) on the horizon.

© Troy Henkels

CHAPTER TWENTY-SIX

IT'S NOT OVER UNTIL IT'S OVER

The Cessna 185 touched down on the soft snow to trigger the roughest small-plane landing I had ever experienced. The plane shook as it rocketed off hidden sastrugi underneath the skis. Jim, our pilot, inspected his landing gear to make sure he hadn't damaged anything after hitting the ridges of hard-packed snow. He needed to take off again. He said if he knew it was going to be that rough, he never would have landed. I believed him.

After 10 years of big, long-haul expeditions all over the world, I found myself with an urge to get back to my roots and into the mountains of Alaska. It had been so long since I'd been on a small, self-driven Alaskan adventure, it seemed I was slowly losing touch with what it was I

Ron and Dave (and Jason) saving the day with their Supercub. © Troy Henkels

really enjoyed. This time, instead of big money, appeasing sponsors, complex logistics, expensive websites, and world travels, I really wanted to do something close to home with a good friend. For most of the winter I looked over maps of Alaska and kept finding myself focusing on the Harding icefield. This mammoth icefield a few hours south of where I live covers roughly 1,000 square miles and spawns over 40 glaciers. With annual snowfall of over 400 inches it seemed like the perfect place for a kiting expedition. It was one place I had always wanted to explore and had never really taken the time to experience. With no big expeditions stealing my focus, this was the perfect time.

Over the course of several weeks, an expedition began to materialize as I considered the short list of friends who were qualified, capable, and possibly interested in this sort of adventure. The plan was to fly to the far end of the icefield, climb one of the big peaks and then use kites to traverse north across the icefield back to a glacier that allowed us an easy departure point. This plan seemed simple and concise enough. It was a trip I had been dreaming about for over 10 years. When I called my friend Jason in Florida to pitch the idea, his response came quickly. He was in. Jason was an old friend whom I met in the paragliding community. He quickly became interested in and competent at kiting, on both snow and water. Although only 25, he had spent enough long days in the mountains to have the necessary skills, to know his limitations, and most importantly, know how to be safe. A year earlier, after graduating from college in Alaska, he had moved to Florida to get his pilot's license and eventually become a flight instructor. Now he was really looking for a reason to get back to Alaska, a place he really loved. It turns out that an expedition to the Harding icefield was all the coaxing he needed.

After six months of emails and phone calls, Jason and I are loading Jim's plane on a brisk Saturday morning for the 45-minute flight to our drop-off point. Both of us are jittery with excitement as the 185 climbs out of Anchorage airspace and over Turnagain Arm and into the Kenai mountains. Jim, is a kiter, too, so he is keen to fly his plane over the icefield and have a closer look to scout out areas for future kiting excursions. In particular, I am interested in seeing our entire route to search for crevasse fields, extremely dangerous areas we hope to avoid. And it is necessary to have a look at the mountains around Exit Glacier, our departure point. With not a cloud in the sky we take in an aerial look at the entire icefield before touching down on a snowy plateau at a high point in the field.

The rough landing has Jason and I flashing glances at each other, wondering what we have gotten into and hoping there is no damage to the airplane. Fortunately, there isn't. After we unload, Jim takes off, headed back to his family in Anchorage. When the plane is out of earshot, the complete silence is deafening. We are ecstatic with the thought of spending nine days with nothing but the sound of the wind. Immediately, we load our gear onto the sleds and start pulling uphill. We want to get to the crest of the slope and figure out our exact position to determine if it is feasible to climb Truuli Peak.

Not five minutes into the pulling, we feel a bit of wind on our faces. We had come here to kite, so we put kites in the air and for the next hour have the time of our lives kiting all around this mammoth plateau.

After the wind dies, we pull out the maps and realize we are actually 20 miles from Truuli Peak. This will mean a diversion of 40 miles, round trip, going in the opposite direction from our route. And that is not counting whatever challenges we might experience getting up the peak. With a forecast of only a few days of nice weather, we both know it is a good decision to strap on the sleds and start pulling toward Exit glacier before bad weather sets in. Even without the Truuli climb, we had a long way to go.

After several hours, it is getting late and we decide to camp for the night – but not before we unclip from the sleds and ski another hour and take in some spectacular nunataks. Climbing to the top of these ridges, we have enough elevation to see a large portion of the icefield and discuss which route will offer the least chance of crevasse danger. The views of this expansive plateau of ice, speckled with jagged peaks all around, has us both searching for words to

Home for the night in the middle of the icefield.

© Troy Henkels

describe their beauty. The route looks relatively crevasse-free and we hope for wind so we can use the kites to cover miles easily. When we finally crawl into our sleeping bags, it is minus-5 degrees Fahrenheit. Perfect sleeping weather.

The next day, dawns clear and windless as predicted. On an expedition like this, packing up camp is no quick task. Finding the motivation to get out of a warm sleeping bag, melt snow for water, have breakfast, break camp, and load the sleds, typically takes about two hours. By 10 a.m. we clip into our sleds and start dragging our 150 pounds of gear across the icefield. After an hour, the wind picks up and, like excited boys, we can't get our kites into the air fast enough. The breeze is only a surface wind and extremely light. Even with our biggest kites (15m and 19m), we can't harness this strange laminar flow of air. The kites will fly until they get about 20 feet off the ground and then fall. We finally realized it is futile. We pack up the kites and continue pulling our sleds.

We are on a slight incline for the next three hours, and the pulling is rough. The surface of hard, wind-packed sastrugi makes our hips burn due to the friction from the pulling harness. But the surface is always variable where there is wind and snow, and for the balance of the day the sleds glide easily on a softer surface with a few inches of new snow. After covering eight miles, we stop for the night. We are surprised to look back and realize we have been going slightly downhill for the last half of the day. It didn't seem to matter which direction we were going, if we were pulling the sleds, it always seemed uphill. A quick check on the topo map confirms that, indeed, we have been mostly going ever-so-slightly downhill.

As we set up camp, it is apparent that it is colder than it was the previous night. The thermometer confirms this: It is minus-20 Fahrenheit! We put on our down clothes and hunker in for a chilly evening. Just after I begin melting snow for our dinner and drinking water, our stove suddenly catches fire and bursts into flames. It is a precarious situation, but we are lucky we have the stove in the tent vestibule and not inside the tent itself. After quickly extinguishing the fire, I light the stove again and it immediately catches fire again. I make a closer inspection and discover an irreparable leak. Jason digs out the back-up stove, which worked for

us the previous night. Now we can't even get it lit! With one quart of water between us and at least three days away from being off the ice field, we are in a predicament. It is not an emergency yet, but it will be one by the same time tomorrow if we can't melt snow for water. While discussing our options, including whether to end the expedition, we are glad we brought a satellite phone. One phone call later to my friend Dave, who is the best bush pilot I know, results in an unhesitating response: "I'll be there by mid-morning." With no hot water, we are at a loss to make our dehydrated dinner. But Jason, in his 25-year-old wisdom, has brought a pound of bacon, several cans of tuna and salmon, and cheese. Despite earlier chiding him for packing such heavy luxuries, I am glad he did as we feast on these delicacies.

By mid-morning the next day I hear a plane coming in low on the horizon. Dave, in a red-and-white SuperCub, lands and parks his plane not 10 feet from our tent. He and his friend Ron drop off two new stoves and give us an updated weather report. With beautiful sunny skies, they are happy to have an excuse to be out flying, despite the cold temperatures. They even have scouted out our potential route for the next couple of days. After they depart, we melt snow for our day's water, pack up camp, and start monotonously dragging our sleds farther across the icefield.

This is to be our last day of sun, and the forecast calls for a low ceiling and limited visibility. We want to make as much headway toward Exit Glacier as possible while we still

Jason pulling hard to get off the icefield.   © Troy Henkels

Jason taking advantage of a light wind with his biggest kite.

have decent weather and good visibility. With absolutely no wind, skiing conditions are perfect for putting in some miles. Distances on the ice are amazingly deceiving. After skiing for six hours, we feel we are no closer than when we started the day. Some of the best Fata Morgana (mirages) that I have ever seen appear and keep the distances illusive. After several more hours of heavy pulling, a light wind starts to blow. Jason puts his kite in the air and is able to finally use it to pull the sled to where we would camp for the night. As daylight fades, we take turns setting up camp while the other kite-skis. All the while we watch a spectacular sunset. The wind eventually dies out and a nearly full moon crests over the distant mountains.

By morning, the mood of the icefield has changed. As predicted, the weather has turned, the light is flat, and there is a very low ceiling of clouds. We can barely make out the peaks that will guide us to our departure point at Exit Glacier three miles away. It takes us two hours to reach land and get off the icefield proper. Our plan is to search for a

trail that traverses down the steep mountainside, one that tourists use in the summer to get a glimpse of the icefield. Our presumption is we will quickly find the trail and the expedition will all but be over except for an easy hike down to sea level. But it is not meant to be.

Climbing several steep slopes, we search for the trail, hauling our 150-pound sleds behind us. This puts us both near the point of exhaustion. After a short break we continue our descent. Before long, we are immersed in a maze of chaotic, near-vertical gulleys and cliffs. Such steep slopes are susceptible to avalanche, and this becomes our primary concern. Being competent skiers pays off for us, and we are able to ski and let our sleds utilize gravity while we find our way down several steep sections. But the more elevation we lose, the warmer, softer, and more avalanche-prone the conditions become. We descend into a steep, narrow gulley and find ourselves committed. With the heavy sleds, there is no turning back from this point. Neither one of us can tell what is below, because it is too steep. Chances are good

that there is a cliff partway down the chute. Scouting the route only tells me that it is doable, but I can't quite see the entire chute. Jason goes first. He almost makes it all the way down before he cuts his sled loose and watches it tumble for several hundred feet down the mountainside. It comes to rest in a gigantic pile of avalanche debris. Without the difficulty of controlling the sled, he skis a chute no wider than four feet, and nearly vertical. He skis all the way to his sled. With crampons on my boots, I follow, and find it to be just as dangerous. I too have to cut my sled loose at the same section. We watch it tumble and roll down the mountain. With a deep breath, we think the worst is over. It isn't.

As we push, pull, and heave our sleds through a wide chute of bizarre avalanche debris, we end up in a slot canyon, hemmed in by 100-foot cliffs on each side of us. I scout a route to get out of the canyon, and I stop short. It ends on top of a cliff over 200 feet high. A beautiful icefall pours off the face of the cliff. It is higher than what I have rope for, and rappelling out of this predicament is not an option. We

have to come up with another plan. The only way out is to climb one of the cliffs in the canyon and begin the arduous process of hauling our gear up the side of the cliff face. This is no easy chore. After climbing up, I set up a 3:1 pulley system and begin the tedious, energy-draining process of pulling up all our gear. In the meantime, Jason makes several laps climbing the cliff, hauling some of the lighter gear. By the time we have everything out of the canyon, I am done and so is Jason. We are both so utterly worn-out from being on the move for 10 hours, most of it grueling work, that we set up camp in a somewhat precarious spot right on top of the cliff and call it a night. After consuming generous portions of food, we sleep like we are dead, exhausted from the day's exertions. Getting down from the icefield has been far more challenging than either of us had anticipated. And we aren't even all the way down yet!

The next morning, we are ready to be off steep terrain and back on level ground. Standing on a narrow ridge with steep cliffs dropping off on both sides, we know this isn't

going to be an easy day. Dragging the sleds across the hill, and sometimes uphill, desperately searching for safe passage off this mountain is a staggering task. We battle through knee and, often, waist-deep snow. When we have gone as far as we can across the hillside, we end up looking down steep cliffs that drop straight onto Exit Glacier.

While scouting which cliff is going to be most feasible to rappel from, I stumble upon a steep snow-filled ramp that skirts the lower part of a cliff and leads all the way to the valley floor, 1,000 feet below. We are home free!

After another hour of exhausting and frustrating work managing the heavy sleds, we at last stand on solid, level ground. We have covered nearly 40 miles in five days without incident or injury. But, it isn't over. There are still seven miles to ski on flat ground to get to a plowed roadway that would take us to the town of Seward and civilization. But this seems like easy going compared to what we have just been through. Jason calls it a "full-on gnarly experience." Absolutely thrashed, all I can do is agree. This expedition turns out to be more challenging than either of us expected.

At home two days later, I called Jason to see how he was recovering from our ordeal. His response came slowly, but assuredly. He said, "Dude, that was a cool trip. When can we go again?" That's all I needed to hear. Before we even hung up the phone, the maps were out, as we contemplated the next great Alaskan adventure.

Scouting out a safe passage from the top of a nunatak.
© Jason Turnbull